W9-CVO-280

The Reference Guide

A Handbook for Office Personnel

Ralph M. Holmes

HOUGHTON MIFFLIN COMPANY / BOSTON
Atlanta   Dallas   Geneva, Illinois
Hopewell, New Jersey   Palo Alto   Toronto

Credits

All illustrations were prepared by ANCO/Boston except for those on pages 93, 103 which were prepared by George Ulrich.

Printed in the U.S.A.

ISBN: 0-395-27252-1

Contents

Preface

The Reference Guide: A Handbook for Office Personnel was developed for two purposes: (1) to serve as a ready reference for students and office workers, and (2) to be used as a teaching/learning/reviewing tool both in the classroom and on an individual study basis.

As a clear and concise ready reference, it provides answers to those questions most frequently encountered in the classroom and the office. Designed to promote rapid location of major topics and related subtopics, *The Reference Guide* enables the user to pinpoint with little effort the specific information sought. The thumb index, table of contents, numbered topics, generally alphabetical arrangement of topics within units, running heads, and index can be used to speed up the location process. The handy size and spiral binding permit easy storage and readability at the desk. The second color highlights the logical numbering and labeling system of the major topics.

As a teaching/learning/reviewing tool, *The Reference Guide* can be used both for directed classroom study and individual study programs. Selected units can be emphasized, or a "mini-course" can be conducted using *The Reference Guide* as the basic text/workbook. Self-check exercises with answers for each unit can be used for self-evaluation, followed by teacher-evaluated exercises, which are provided for duplication in the Teacher's Manual.

Most rules and narrative statements are followed by examples for clarity. Numerous sources were referred to in checking the accuracy of statements and rules. Where differences of opinion exist, some attempt was made to follow the most common interpretation; however, some statement regarding the various alternatives generally accompanies such interpretations.

In addition to coverage of items ordinarily expected in reference manuals, the following were included to increase the usefulness of *The Reference Guide:* a list of commonly misspelled words, with word division points; a glossary of important business terms; a brief discussion of basic business forms, accompanied by illustrations; a list of typing tips and shortcuts; a brief discussion of the most common filing rules; and a comprehensive unit on seeking employment.

Appreciation is expressed to those companies and organizations who gave assistance in preparation of the manuscript and in the sharing of information as well as to those individuals who read the manuscript and made suggestions and contributions.

R.M.H.

1 Punctuation

PUNCTUATION helps the writer give expression to what is written and helps the reader understand what is read. Without punctuation, sentences and paragraphs would be a jumble of words, and written communication would be impossible.

While exceptions do exist, the following punctuation rules are the most commonly used.

APOSTROPHE

Use an apostrophe

1.1 To show possession.
   a. Add an apostrophe and s ('s) to singular nouns or plural nouns not ending in s.

   The office manager's office is near the elevator.
   Children's clothes are sold only on the first floor of the store.

   b. Add an apostrophe and s ('s) to a proper name.

   James's training lasted for six months.
   We are invited to the Wallis's home for a celebration.

   c. Add only an apostrophe (') after plural nouns ending in s.

   The managers' conference was very successful.

   d. Add an apostrophe and s ('s) to the final noun only to show joint possession.

   It was Winston and Cartwright's first novel together.

1.2 To indicate the omission of letters in contractions or figures.

   I couldn't and wouldn't dampen the class enthusiasm.
   The tenth reunion of the class of '71 was held that year.

1.3 To form the plural of words used as words, figures, letters, and abbreviations with periods.

We inserted the's, and's, and that's in the letter.
Check the 5's; they look too much like 6's.
Her name is spelled with two t's.
Paul and Maria received their M.B.A.'s from Harvard.

There is a trend to eliminate the apostrophe in some plurals.

9s   1970s

1.4 To indicate feet or minutes.

The office measured 48' by 72'.
She finished the race in 4'.

1.5 As single quotation marks for a quotation within a quotation.

The instructor asked, "Have you read the article 'Offices of the Future' as you were assigned?"

1.6 Do not space before or after an apostrophe used within a word. Leave one space after, but not before, an apostrophe that appears at the end of a word.

ASTERISK

Use an asterisk

1.7 To indicate a footnote that appears at the bottom of a page.

Steven* Foster was a gentle person.

_____

*Sometimes spelled Stephen.

1.8 To indicate the omission of an unprintable word.

The child, being born out of wedlock, was called a ***.

1.9 To indicate the omission of a complete paragraph.

in the majority of cases.
* * *
When the tests were resumed, it was found that 43 percent

1.10 If an asterisk is used as a footnote reference within the text, leave one space after the asterisk. If it falls at the end of a sentence, leave two spaces. In the footnote itself, do not space after the asterisk.

If asterisks show the omission of an unprintable word, use three asterisks with no space between them.

To show the omission of a complete paragraph, use three asterisks, centered on the line of type with one space between.

BRACE
Use a brace

1.11 As a joining device in legal matters.

James Benson   )
   Plaintiff   )

     vs.   )

Raymond Brown   )
   Defendant   )

1.12 On a typewriter, a brace is made by joining two or more right parentheses.

BRACKETS
Use brackets

1.13 To show editorial corrections.

The League of Nations [United Nations] furnished peace-keeping troops.

1.14 To indicate an error or questionable word in written material by inserting [sic].

He said that the stationary [sic] would be delivered today.

1.15 For insertions made by someone other than the author or speaker.

The defendant swore the accident occurred at the corner of West and Summer Streets [West and Summer Streets do not intersect].

1.16 To enclose material within material already in parentheses.

(She referred him to Historical Writings [3d edition], p. 27.)

1.17 Brackets, like parentheses, should be closed up to the material they enclose. Leave one space before the left bracket and one space after the right bracket.

1.18 If your typewriter does not have brackets, they can be made as follows:

a. To type the left bracket, strike the diagonal key, backspace, and strike the underscore key. Roll the paper back one line and strike the underscore key again. Begin typing the enclosed material immediately after the diagonal.
b. To type the right bracket, strike the underscore key (under the last letter typed) and the diagonal, then backspace. Roll the paper back one line and strike the underscore key again.

Brackets can also be drawn in by hand. If you choose to do so, leave space before and after the material to be enclosed. Draw the brackets, in ink, when the paper is removed from the typewriter.

COLON

Use a colon

1.19 To introduce a listing that follows.

The office manager ordered the following: five reams of paper, eight packages of tape, and two boxes of typewriter ribbons.

1.20 To separate hours and minutes in expressions of time.

6:45 a.m.   10:01 p.m.

1.21 In proportions.

4:1   3:2

1.22 After salutations in business letters using mixed punctuation.

Dear Mr. Riley: Ladies and Gentlemen:

1.23 To separate the writer's initials from the typist's in reference initials.

JRG:orb

1.24 In footnotes and bibliography entries to separate the city of publication from the publisher's name.

²Rodger Whitley, *On Trying Harder* (New York: Wilson Publishing Co., 1979), p. 16.

Whitley, Rodger. *On Trying Harder.* New York: Wilson Publishing Co., 1979.

1.25 Do not space before or after a colon used in expressions of time, proportions, or reference initials.

In all other cases, leave two spaces after a colon; do not space before.

1.26 A colon should always appear outside quotation marks or parentheses.

COMMA

Use a comma

1.27 To set off academic degrees and seniority titles following a person's name.

Willa Johnson, Ph.D.   Ronald Williams, Sr.
Kyle Martin, III
Arnold Goldman, Doctor of Laws, presided at the meeting.
She nominated John Hunt, Jr., as treasurer.

1.28 Between two or more adjectives preceding and modifying the same noun.

The report listed the large, outstanding debts of the firm.
The tall, thin, spindly trees waved in the strong wind.

1.29 To set off appositives. An *appositive* is a word that explains or describes the noun or pronoun it follows.

Ms. Chung, my supervisor, told me that I would get a raise.
The receptionist, Andy Youngblood, does a good job of meeting the
    public.
It was she, the payroll clerk, who made the error in my check.

1.30 After the complimentary close in letters using mixed punctuation.

Yours truly,   Sincerely,

1.31 To separate the parts in dates and addresses.

Helen Marie Anderson was born on April 13, 1933.
Her address is 3807 Winston Drive, Bellvue, Massachusetts.
On Monday, March 23, 1977, the word processing center opened.

1.32 In direct address.

Complete the job, John, and complete it on time.
Maureen, will you get this letter in the mail this morning?
Will you prepare the report for the committee, Paul?

1.33 To set off direct quotations.

The receptionist said, "You may go in now."

"It is just a matter of time," the supervisor said, "until you receive a
   promotion."
"The customer is always right," said the executive.

1.34 To set off the abbreviation "etc."

The box contained paper clips, rubber bands, pins, staples, etc.
She brought tablets, pens, pencils, etc., to the meeting.

1.35 To set off the words "Inc." and "Ltd." in company names.

Warren Company, Inc.   Jaubert, Ltd.
Market Research, Inc., sent the report to the president.

1.36 To separate the items in a series.

Mr. Wilson hired Rhonda, Harry, and Beth for the office staff.
Mrs. Ramirez has either 23, 24, or 25 students in her class.

1.37 To separate thousands and millions in numbers of four or more digits.

26,011   375,678,431

1.38 To separate two numbers in succession to avoid confusion.

In all there were 14, 11 of which were faulty.

1.39 To show the omission of words.

The typists sent flowers; the secretaries, candy.
I'll do most of the work today; tomorrow, the rest.

1.40 To set off parenthetical expressions and nonrestrictive phrases and
clauses. Parenthetical expressions and nonrestrictive phrases and
clauses are words, phrases, or clauses that could be omitted without
changing the meaning of the sentence.

You were told, however, that the job would not be easy.
Mr. Suter, for example, has worked for the company ten years.
The company benefits, I believe, are more than generous.

1.41 To separate the surname from the rest of the name in transposed
names.

Jones, Kyle W.   Jovan, Elizabeth W.

1.42 Before coordinating conjunctions (*and, but, for, or, nor*) in compound
sentences.

The reports were completed today, and they will be mailed tomorrow.

Tim received the assignment weeks ago, but he has not completed it
   yet.
He did not get a raise, for his work had not been acceptable.
Let us work quickly, or we will not be able to finish today.
I will never be late, nor will I do less than my best.

1.43 To set off introductory words and phrases in sentences.

Yes, I said that I would take responsibility for the failure.
Consequently, we completed our work in time for the holidays.
In just a few days, the filing system began to work effectively.

1.44 To set off introductory dependent clauses in sentences.

If the report is completed today, we can take tomorrow off.
After the sales report was made, the officers held a special meeting.
When the training program is completed, we will receive certificates.

1.45 Do not space before a comma; leave one space after. Do not space
before or after a comma if it is used to separate thousands and/or
millions within a number.

1.46 Always place a comma inside quotations marks. If a comma is used
with parentheses or brackets, place it outside.

DASH

Use a dash

1.47 For emphasis when a sudden change occurs in the sentence.

It was just yesterday—or was it Friday—that she called.

1.48 To emphasize a parenthetical expression.

Miss Johnson—an outstanding teacher—recommended further training.
The masterpiece—a Rembrandt—was displayed in a prominent location.

1.49 Before an author's name that follows a quotation.

A penny saved is a penny earned.—Franklin

1.50 Do not space before or after a dash.

1.51 In typewritten material, the dash is made by typing two hyphens.

DIAGONAL

Use a diagonal

1.52 Between two words to indicate that either or both may be used in the sentence.

The assignment was to retype the report and/or file the letters.

1.53 To separate the numbers in the short form of a date.

1/1/80

1.54 Between two numbers or letters to express a fraction, an abbreviation, or a period of time.

The report was 4 1/3 pages.
Send the letters c/o William Bradley.
The report was for 1978/79.

1.55 Do not space before or after a diagonal.

ELLIPSIS

Use an ellipsis

1.56 To indicate an intentional omission of one or more words in quoted material.

"To be or not to be . . . whether it be nobler in the hearts of men."
"I am sorry I have but one life to give. . . ."

1.57 When an ellipsis indicates an omission within a sentence, use three periods, with one space before, between, and after each period.
    When an ellipsis falls at the end of a sentence, use four periods. However, the first period should immediately follow the preceding word.

EXCLAMATION POINT

Use an exclamation point

1.58 To express strong feelings or a command.

You've just won the prize!
Stop! Don't press that switch!

1.59 Leave two spaces after the exclamation point at the end of a sentence; do not space before it.

1.60 Place an exclamation point inside the quotation mark only if it is part of the quoted material. If it is not part of the quoted material, place an exclamation point outside the quotation mark.

1.61 If your typewriter does not have an exclamation point key, you can make one as follows: Strike the apostrophe key, backspace, and strike the period key.

HYPHEN
Use a hyphen

1.62 To join the elements of a compound adjective before the noun it modifies.

It was a first-class operation.

1.63 In compound numbers from 21 to 99 that are spelled out.

seventy-nine   one thousand thirty-four

1.64 To show that two or more compound words share the same base.

The supervisor quoted first-, second-, and third-class rates.

1.65 With inclusive dates and numbers.

January 10-12, 1980   14-16 cases
1978-1980   pages 1-4

1.66 To divide a word between syllables at the end of a line.

The traffic officer said that he had not seen such a monumental traffic jam.

1.67 With spelled-out fractions used as adjectives.

one-half share   two-thirds vote

1.68 To join certain prefixes to words.

ex-officio   self-denial
great-grandfather   all-inclusive

1.69 To separate a prefix from a proper noun.

pro-Canada   ex-Dolphin

1.70 Do not space before or after a hyphen used within a word or number.

PARENTHESES
Use parentheses

1.71 To set off expressions that clarify or further explain a part of a sentence.

The FTC (*Federal Trade Commission*) ruled that the advertising was misleading.

1.72 To set off dollar amounts in legal and business documents.

The party of the first part agrees to pay Five Hundred Dollars ($500).

1.73 To indicate enumerated items in a sentence.

To be promoted you must have: (1) a college degree, (2) three years of experience, and (3) good ratings from your supervisor.

1.74 In footnotes, to set off the place of publication, the publisher, and the date.

[1]Marleen Davis, *Windmills of My Mind* (San Francisco: Riley Publishers, 1980), p. 216.
[3]Anne G. Mayes, "The Nashville Experiment," *Business Exchange* 1 (April 1979), pp. 3-4.

1.75 To set off periods of time.

The Civil War period (1861-1865) was a difficult time for the country.

1.76 Leave one space before the left parenthesis and one space after the right parenthesis.

1.77 If another punctuation mark appears and applies to the complete sentence rather than the material enclosed in parentheses, place it *outside* the right parenthesis.

If the punctuation mark applies to the material enclosed in parentheses, place it inside the right parenthesis.

PERIOD

Use a period

1.78 After a declarative sentence.

The rain ended by late afternoon.

1.79 After an imperative sentence.

Come to my office immediately.

1.80 After a simple request.

Will you please respond to my letter.

1.81 After initials, academic degrees, and abbreviations.

J. R. R. Tolkien	Ronald T. Wilkins, Ph.D.
Co.	Jan.
f.o.b.	Ms. Susan Smialek

1.82 As a decimal point in dollar amounts, decimals, or percentages.

$27.50	0.1416
47.5%	

1.83 After the numbers and letters in outlines.

    I. xxxxx
       A. xxxxx
       B. xxxxx
          1. xxxxx
          2. xxxxx
             a. xxxxx
             b. xxxxx

1.84 Leave two spaces after a period at the end of a sentence or in enumerated outlines.

Leave one space after the period at the end of an abbreviation or initial unless it falls at the end of a sentence.

Do not space after a period used as a decimal point or within an abbreviation.

1.85 Always place a period inside quotation marks except when single quotation marks are used to set off a special term. A period is also placed inside an asterisk at the end of a sentence.

When material enclosed in parentheses or brackets appears at the end of a sentence, place the period outside the right parenthesis or bracket. If a complete, independent sentence is enclosed in parentheses or brackets, place the period inside the right parenthesis or bracket.

QUESTION MARK

Use a question mark

1.86 After a direct question.

Have you received the answer to his letter?

1.87 To express doubt.

The president is dead (?).
It was an extremely interesting (?) lecture.

1.88 To indicate several short questions within one sentence.

Do you know the time? the place? the cost?

1.89 Leave two spaces after a question mark at the end of a sentence. Leave one space after a question mark within a sentence. Do not space before or after a question mark enclosed in parentheses and used to express doubt.

1.90 Place a question mark inside quotation marks, parentheses, or brackets only when it is part of the quoted or enclosed material.

QUOTATION MARKS

Use quotation marks

1.91 To enclose a direct quotation.

"We will arrive at noon," Betty said.
"When," Bob asked, "do you plan to leave?"

Quotations of more than one paragraph have a quotation mark at the beginning of each paragraph and at the end of the last quoted paragraph.

1.92 To refer to a word itself rather than what it represents.

He felt the word "nuclear" was hard to pronounce.

1.93 To enclose a definition or a foreign word.

That abbreviation means "in the same place."
"Livre" is the French word for book.

1.94 To indicate irony.

The "discussion" ended in a name-calling session.

1.95 To enclose titles of articles, speeches, and chapters of books.

The assignment was to read "To the Sea in Ships."
Mary's speech, "You Begin at the Bottom," was well received.
You are to read Chapter 5, "The Perfect Letter," for tomorrow's class.

1.96 Leave one space before the left quotation mark and one space after the right quotation mark unless it falls at the end of a sentence.

1.97 Always place quotation marks outside a period or comma.

"Get this in the mail today," the manager said, "or it will be late."

Always place the quotation marks inside the colon or semicolon.

He stated his "creed": Look out for number one.
She set the "quota"; we did our best to reach it.

Exclamation points and question marks are placed inside the quotation marks if they are actually part of the quoted material. Otherwise, they are placed outside the quotation marks.

The typist asked, "How many copies should I make?"
Did he say, "Her work is not good enough"?
After seeing the financial report, the manager exclaimed, "Wow!"
You'll have to hurry if you want to catch the "express"!

SEMICOLON

Use a semicolon

1.98 To separate two or more independent clauses in a compound sentence not joined by a conjunction.

The financial statement was completed; the report to the stockholders was prepared.
We will prepare the stencils; they will duplicate the report.

1.99 Between the clauses of a compound sentence when they are joined by a conjunctive adverb such as *accordingly, consequently, hence, however, in fact, moreover, nevertheless, therefore, thus, whereas,* and *yet.*

The job must be finished this week; consequently, we will work over-
time.
She did the best job she could; nevertheless, it was not good enough.
Miss Jones interviewed all the candidates; thus, she was able to
select the best qualified candidate.

Note the comma following these connecting words in the sentences
above.

1.100 Between the clauses of a compound sentence if either clause contains
a comma.

William typed the reports, letters, and memos; and he was always
busy.
Mr. Doud reported an upswing in business; but he reminded us of the
inefficiency, waste, and disorganization that still existed.

1.101 Between parts of a listing when there are commas within the parts.

She received the following: three invoices, each marked paid; five
statements, one containing an error; and three letters, each with her
name misspelled.

1.102 Leave one space after, but not before, a semicolon.

1.103 Place a semicolon outside quotation marks, parentheses, or brackets.

UNDERSCORE

Use the underscore

1.104 To emphasize a word.

You have too many <u>and's</u> in your paragraphs.

1.105 To indicate the title of a book, magazine, or newspaper.

The title of the book was <u>Some Went to War</u>.
She subscribed to <u>Time</u>, a weekly news magazine.
Lennie Martin delivers the <u>Daily Globe</u> to our house.

1.106 To indicate italics in material to be set in type by a printer.

Many people misspell <u>receive</u>.

1.107 An underscore should be typed as a solid line and should not appear
under other punctuation marks that are not part of the underscored
material.

Self-Check Exercise

Supply the correct punctuation in the following memo.

TO: Marilyn Flescher Budget Director

FROM: Richard Riley Regional Sales Manager

DATE: January 16 1980

SUBJECT: Evaluation Salaries and Bonuses

After the recent sales conference Mr Wilson the National Sales Manager asked each regional sales office to present ideas for improvement in the following areas 1 evaluation 2 salaries and 3 bonuses He also asked that our ideas be reported no later than February 15 1980 The purpose of this memo Marilyn is to secure specific concise information that will help me complete the report

In his address to the conference Mr Wilson said We need accurate data to ensure that each representatives work is evaluated fairly Since this is the case I wonder if you can supply me with a copy of the incentive plan or is it referred to as the bonus plan which you presented at the conference Did your report include employees covered employee cost company cost

Can you also supply me with first second and third quarter salary and bonus figures for those employees assigned to our regional office I suspect that these figures for example will clearly show that over 35 representatives exceeded $20000 in salary and bonuses

In a recent issue of Financial Weekly an article entitled Bonuses and Employee Morale insisted there was a direct positive correlation between the two In discussions with other regional managers the same correlation was indicated nevertheless I am not sure this is always true Perhaps the information you supply to me will change my mind Seeing is believing Horatio

Check your answers in the back of the book.

2 Capitalization

CAPITALIZATION is based, for the most part, on a set of well-established and accepted rules. Sometimes, however, it is used for emphasis and clarification and may not observe strict rules. The most commonly accepted and widely used capitalization rules follow.

ACADEMIC DEGREES

2.1 Capitalize specific academic degrees, whether spelled out or abbreviated.

Cynthia Graebo, Ph.D., was named to the position by the school.
Brent Spencer, Doctor of Philosophy, will deliver the commencement address.
Lionel received his bachelor's degree last year.

ARMED FORCES

2.2 Capitalize the names of the specific branches of the armed forces.

U.S. Army	National Guard
U.S. Navy	U.S. Coast Guard
the Marine Corps	Air National Guard

ASTRONOMICAL AND CELESTIAL BODIES

2.3 Capitalize the names of planets, stars, constellations, and other celestial bodies, except for *earth, sun,* and *moon.* Capitalize the word "earth" only when used with other capitalized celestial bodies.

the Milky Way	Mercury
Orion	Rigel

We studied the similarities of Earth and Mars in the class.

BEGINNING WORDS

2.4 Capitalize the beginning word of a sentence.

Energy conservation is important to us all.
Why must we be so cost conscious?
The wind blew the top off the house!

2.5 Capitalize the beginning word of a quotation unless it is a fragmentary quotation or is closely woven into the sentence.

The instructor asked, "Have you completed your reports?"
The sales manager said that we would "make our annual quota."
"If you have ever climbed a mountain," he said, " you know the meaning of a challenge."

2

2.6 Capitalize the first word after a colon only if a complete sentence follows.

He gave two reasons: declining sales and increased costs.
There were two reasons for her failing: She did not study, and she had personal problems.

2.7 Capitalize the beginning word of phrases meant to stand alone.

Now, to get to the point.
What a relief!

2.8 Capitalize the beginning word of lines of poetry.

I think that I shall never see
A poem lovely as a tree.
                    Joyce Kilmer

2.9 Capitalize the beginning word and other important words of divisions of outlines.

I. Business Typing
    A. Letters
    B. Forms
    C. Legal Documents

BUSINESS NAMES

2.10 Capitalize all important words in business names. Do not capitalize *the, and, of,* and other such words unless they are the first word of the business name.

National Tool and Die Company   Inn on the Sea
Tom's Meat Market   The Racquetball Club
Talk of the Town Lounge   Capitol Auditing Service

2.11 Do not capitalize the words "company" and "corporation" used in place of the full name.

Every employee of the company is covered by medical insurance.

COMPASS POINTS

2.12 Capitalize points of the compass only when they designate specific locations. Do *not* capitalize when they are used simply to indicate direction.

The driest weather occurs in the West and Southwest.
Tammy grew up in a small town in the Middle West.
The ice storm struck the northern part of the state.
We plan to hike south of the river to arrive at South Peak.

DATES

2.13 Capitalize days of the week, months of the year, and holidays.

The office will be closed for Thanksgiving on Thursday and Friday.
Our busiest months are January, February, and March.

2.14 Do not capitalize names of the seasons unless using personification.

In the eastern section of the country, winter is usually cold and snowy; summer is warm and pleasant.
"Ah, Spring, thy touch is so tender."

ETHNIC AND RACIAL REFERENCES

2.15 Capitalize terms that relate to ethnic groups, cultures, languages, or races.

Chinese	English
Caucasian	Spanish
German	Arabic
Indian	Orientals

2.16 Do not capitalize the words "black" and "white."

GEOGRAPHICAL NAMES

2.17 Capitalize names of specific continents, countries, states, cities, towns, streets, mountains, bodies of water, and so on.

the Mississippi River	the Atlantic Ocean
Cincinnati, Ohio	North America
Boston Harbor	United States
Fifth Avenue	the Rocky Mountains
Walden Pond	

2.18 Do not capitalize generic terms such as *river, ocean, city,* and so on, when used alone, when they appear before the proper noun, or when they appear with two or more proper nouns.

> The class studied the Mississippi River and other great rivers of the world.
> We visited harbors in the states of Maryland, Massachusetts, and New York.
> The ship crossed both the Atlantic and Pacific oceans.

GOVERNMENT AND POLITICAL UNITS

2.19 Capitalize the names of specific governmental, political, and judicial units.

the Congress of the United States	the Supreme Court
the United States Senate	Federal Trade Commission
the California Legislature	Cincinnati City Council
	Democratic Party

2.20 Do not capitalize the words "federal," "state," and "government" unless they are part of a proper noun.

> In this country, state governments usually include two houses of a legislature.
> Because it was a national holiday, all federal employees had the day off.

HISTORICAL PERIODS AND EVENTS

2.21 Capitalize the names of historical, cultural, and geological periods.

Stone Age	Middle Ages
Industrial Revolution	Roaring Twenties

2.22 Capitalize the names of all important events.

Boston Tea Party	Civil War
War of 1812	Louisiana Purchase

2.23 Do not capitalize references to centuries or decades.

twentieth century	the seventies

2.24 Capitalize the names of historic documents, treaties, acts, and laws.

Declaration of Independence	U.S. Constitution
Monroe Doctrine	Treaty of Versailles
Taft-Hartley Act	the Eighteenth Amendment

2.25 Do not capitalize references to pending legislation.

Congress is considering a gun-control law.

HYPHENATED WORDS

2.26 Capitalize the proper nouns or proper adjectives found in hyphenated words.

anti-American   Governor-elect Whitley
pre-Civil War   mid-April holiday

LETTER PARTS

2.27 Capitalize the first and other important words in salutations, attention lines, subject lines, and complimentary closes.

Dear Ms. Rodriquez: Ladies and Gentlemen:
Attention: Mr. D. W. Jones   Subject: Invoice No. 1746
Sincerely yours,

NOUNS WITH NUMBERED OR LETTERED ITEMS

2.28 Generally, capitalize a noun appearing before a number or letter.

Flight 430   Catalogue 47
Appendix T   Room 36
Section 7   Code 13
She showed the customer Invoice No. 6337, which covered today's
    shipment.

2.29 Do not capitalize such minor divisions as page, paragraph, line, and verse references.

Turn to page 7, paragraph 3, line 8 to get the correct answer.

ORGANIZATIONS

2.30 Capitalize the important words in names of organizations, institutions, schools, clubs, and so on.

Young Democrats of America   American Artists' Guild
Boston Symphony Orchestra   New York University
Yellow River High School   First Baptist Church
Shalom Temple   University of Wisconsin

PROPER NOUNS AND ADJECTIVES

2.31 Capitalize proper nouns and proper adjectives. Proper nouns are words that name a specific person, place or thing. Proper adjectives are words that describe that name.

Willard T. Jackson	Toledo, Ohio
Washington Monument	London
Fort Knox	the Boston Celtics
Marxist doctrine	Shakespearian plays

2.32 Capitalize surnames exactly as the individual prefers. Foreign surnames do not consistently follow a pattern of capitalization.

MacMillan	LaCoste
de la Fontaine	DeMille
Larose	Van Hagen
Vandergriff	von Ribbentrop

2.33 Do not capitalize words derived from proper nouns that have taken on common usage.

scotch whiskey	china platter
turkish rug	baked alaska
french dressing	plaster of paris

PUBLISHED MATERIALS

2.34 Capitalize the principal words in titles of published materials—books, plays, magazines, newspapers, articles, poems, and lectures.

Moby Dick	*The Grapes of Wrath*
The Wall Street Journal	*Newsweek*
Field and Stream	*The Boston Herald American*

"Growing Up Today," an article by H. M. Hanson, appeared in the latest issue of *The Psychologist*.

In our literature class, we memorized "The Village Blacksmith," a poem by Longfellow.

RELIGIOUS TERMS

2.35 Capitalize names of deities and saints, titles and divisions of sacred writings, names of sacred and holy days, and religious groups.

God
Jesus
the Holy Spirit
the Bible
Genesis
Christmas
Christians
Seventh-Day Adventists

Buddha
the Almighty
St. Matthew
the Koran
Old Testament
Yom Kippur
Baptists

SCHOOL SUBJECTS AND COURSES

2.36 Capitalize titles of specific school courses, but not the names of academic subject areas unless they contain a proper noun.

Her schedule included English I, Home Economics II, Government in Our Society, and Typewriting III.
A good background in mathematics and science is essential for success in engineering.
She took courses in health, physical education, and English.

TITLES

2.37 Capitalize civil, family, military, nobility, professional, and religious titles only if the title immediately precedes a person's name, or is used in place of the name, or is in direct address.

President John F. Kennedy
Uncle Paul
General Ulysses S. Grant
Lord North
Dr. John Clow
Rabbi Wiseman

Mayor White
the Kittle sisters
King Henry VIII
Professor Peter Sterling
Pope John Paul II

Harry Wilson, a general in the army, is my uncle.
Will you see me tomorrow, Doctor?
Elizabeth became queen of England.
We met with Maestro Schilling before the concert.
Ladies and gentlemen, the President of the United States.

2.38 Capitalize honorific titles and forms of address.

His Majesty
Your Honor

Your Royal Highness
Excellency

TRADEMARKS AND BRAND NAMES

2.39 Capitalize words registered as trademarks and specific brand names.

Jell-O   Vaseline
Xerox   Coca Cola
Kellogg's Corn Flakes   Seal's Ice Cream

2.40 Certain trademarks and brand names are no longer protected and need not be capitalized.

nylon   zipper
milk of magnesia   aspirin

Self-Check Exercise

Indicate the proper capitalization in the following sentences by circling the letter to be capitalized.

Example: john andrews said, "our plan is to purchase the cook company on january 5, 1985."

1. she received her doctor's degree from columbia university in 1975.
2. after serving in the air national guard, he worked for langley's department store as a department manager.
3. jennifer, who grew up in the middle west, viewed the harbor at boston with amazement.
4. consider this: rice *must* be imported if india is to survive.
5. the united states senate, before adjourning for memorial day, declared that all federal employees would receive an extra day off.
6. the national business club asked that we send a copy of catalogue 83.
7. the article, "today's inflation, tomorrow's recession," appeared in the *chicago herald* on sunday, january 15, 1973.
8. "while you were in school," ms. andrews asked, "did you take typing, english, and home economics?"
9. my uncle, larry white, was a general in the spanish-american war.
10. in astronomy II, we studied the similarities of saturn and earth.
11. each member of the company had attended the university.
12. his brother, general rudolph, read a chapter from the bible every day.
13. "do you think," he asked, "that we will have to memorize the entire poem?"
14. the government will require all goods from china, mexico, and hungary to be inspected except for turkish rugs.
15. my boss, the general manager, said there would be a mid-july holiday.

Check your answers in the back of the book.

3 Numbers

WRITERS are often faced with the decision of whether to express a number in figures or in words. The following are generally accepted rules for expressing numbers in business.

3

GENERAL RULES

3.1 Spell out numbers up to and including ten. Use figures for numbers over ten.

The company hired two secretaries, six typists, and seven clerks.
They used 16 reams of paper in the job.
The population of the town was 3,467.

3.2 Within a short section of text, treat all numbers in the same category consistently. If the largest number is written in figures, use figures for all.

There were 9 graduates in philosophy, 98 in English, and 364 in business.

3.3 Always spell out a number that begins a sentence. If spelling the number is awkward because of its size, rewrite the sentence to eliminate the number as the first word.

Fourteen hundred file folders were used to house the correspondence.
Forty-one percent of the graduates obtained jobs in the city.
AWKWARD: One thousand six hundred thirty-five new jobs were created by the new petroleum company.
REWRITTEN: The new petroleum company created 1,635 new jobs.

3.4 Spell out approximate numbers and even hundreds, thousands, and millions.

The employee had about fifty days to complete the job.
The company made four hundred thousand boxes during the year.

3.5 Express very large round numbers in figures and units of millions or billions.

176 million   1.4 billion

3.6 Regardless of their size, always use figures with abbreviations or symbols.

47%   4 × 3 = 12
10 ft.   37 m

3.7 Use a comma in numbers of four or more digits.

3,067   157,000
1,385,758

However, when using the metric system, do not use the comma to separate groups of numbers. Instead, leave one space between groups of three numbers.

4 720 525   0.528 75

3.8 When two related numbers appear together, spell out the smaller number and use figures for the larger number.

The manager ordered 300 four-page carbon sets.
Mr. Hopkins said he would need four 200-page notebooks.

3.9 Use a comma to separate unrelated adjacent numbers written in figures.

By the year 1981, 724 new customers had been added.

ADDRESSES

3.10 Use figures to designate state, federal, and interstate highways.

During the trip, we traveled on U.S. 50, State Route 37, and Interstate 71.

3.11 Spell out names of numbered streets up to and including ten. Use ordinal figures for numbered streets over ten.

Eighth Avenue   42nd Street
East 116th Street

3.12 Use figures for house and building numbers, with the exception of *One.*

308 Peakham Road   7023 Paddison Road
6 Redwood Boulevard   One Beacon Street

3.13 Always use figures for ZIP Codes (separated from the state name by one space).

Boston, MA 02107   Cincinnati, OH 45230

DATES AND TIMES

3.14 In correspondence, use figures for the date.

May 16, 1980   27 August 1980 (military usage)
We received your letter on May 19.

3.15 The short form of the date is sometimes used for datelines in interoffice communications and in some general office typing.

5/14/80   5-14-80

3.16 In informal writings, the full number of a year may be abbreviated.

The class of '78 had high hopes for the future.
The old historian said that he remembered the winter of '98.

3.17 Use figures for year dates preceded or followed by era designations. "B.C." ("before Christ") follows the year; "A.D." (*anno Domini*, "in the year of the Lord") precedes the year.

476 B.C.   A.D. 1066

3.18 In legal documents dates may be spelled out or expressed in figures with ordinals.

WITNESSETH this sixteenth day of December, nineteen hundred
    eighty.
WITNESSETH this 16th day of December, 1980.

3.19 Spell out references to centuries and decades.

the twentieth century   the twenties

3.20 In general, spell out the time of day except when stating the exact time. Always spell out the time when using *o'clock*.

It was nearly seven when I reached home.
The workers are expected to be at their desks by nine o'clock.
The thermostat is lowered at precisely 2:39 each day.

3.21 Always use figures with a.m. or p.m.

The messenger will arrive at 9:00 a.m. to pick up the report; it must be
    delivered by 2:30 p.m.

Never use the words "evening," "morning," "afternoon," or "o'clock" with a.m. or p.m.

3.22 In the 24-hour military system of time, use figures without the a.m. or p.m.

0830 (8:30 a.m.)   1629 (4:29 p.m.)

DECIMALS, FRACTIONS, AND PERCENTAGES

3.23 Always use figures for decimal numbers. Decimal fractions should always be preceded by a zero.

Statistics show that the average length of time spent on the job was 2.3 years.
The figure of 0.375 was obtained by the accountant.

3.24 A series of fractions in a sentence is best understood when expressed in figures.

The heirs received $\frac{1}{8}$, $\frac{1}{4}$, and $\frac{1}{6}$ of the proceeds of the sale of the property.

3.25 Use figures for mixed numbers (numbers made up of whole numbers and fractions).

The price of the stock was quoted at $116\frac{2}{3}$ after having been $115\frac{5}{8}$ for two days.

3.26 Hyphenate spelled-out fractions used as adjectives. When used as nouns, write the fractions as two words.

Each of the three will receive a one-third share.
The typist completed one half of the work that day.

3.27 Use figures for percentages, with either the percent symbol % or the word "percent."

The bonds carried interest rates of 7%, 8%, and 11%.
The store will allow a 7 percent discount on cash purchases.

3.28 If the percent number must be spelled out (because it begins a sentence, for example), always use the word "percent."

Nine percent of those graduating got jobs immediately.

GOVERNMENT DESIGNATIONS

3.29 Spell out, in ordinal form, numbers used with specific governments, dynasties, and governing bodies.

Third Reich   Sixteenth Dynasty
Ninth Republic

3.30 In political subdivisions, spell out, in ordinal form, numbers less than 100.

Third Circuit Court   Eighteenth Precinct
Ninth Congressional District   Sixth Ward
Eighty-second Congress

3.31 Spell out, in ordinal form, numbers less than 100 used in military units.

Third Army   Sixty-seventh Regiment
Second 'Battalion, 146th Infantry

MONEY

3.32 Use figures for sums of money (with a dollar sign).

The invoice was for $932.16, of which $296.16 applies to parts.

3.33 Use a combination of figures and words for very large amounts of money.

$146 million $17 billion

3.34 Do not use a decimal point or ciphers (.00) with whole dollar amounts unless they appear with other sums that include both dollars and cents.

The artist received $90 for the portrait.
Lawrence paid $20.00, while Sally paid $17.50.

3.35 For sums of money less than $1, use figures and the word "cents." Do not use the dollar sign or decimal point.

Out of each dollar contributed, 15 cents goes for administration.

3.36 In legal documents, amounts of money are expressed in both words and figures.

. . . to be paid the sum of Twelve Hundred Dollars ($1,200).

ORGANIZATIONS

3.37 Spell out all numbers, in ordinal form, that appear before religious organizations.

First United Methodist Church   Seventh-Day Adventists

3.38 Use figures for numbers designating local branches of unions and fraternal organizations.

Typographical Union No. 73   American Legion Post No. 133

PLURALS OF NUMBERS

3.39 Plurals of spelled-out numbers are formed like other nouns.

The dress shop had a full stock of sixes and sevens.

3.40 To form the plurals of numbers written in figures, add 's. However, current usage favors the addition of an s only.

The tabulation had a number of 6's and 7's.
The bowler had scored many 298s in her career.

PUBLISHED MATERIALS

3.41 Use figures for numbers of pages, chapters, volumes, etc. Capitalized Roman numerals are often used for major divisions of a book.

The information was found on page 116 of Volume 2, Unit IX, Chapter 6.

QUANTITIES AND MEASUREMENTS

3.42 Spell out approximate ages (year only). Use figures for exact age (year, month, day).

His mother is almost seventy-eight years old.
Her son is 3 years, 8 months, and 6 days old.

3.43 Use figures for distances unless indicating fractional quantities.

The marathon was 26 miles 660 feet long.
The runner collapsed one-half mile from the finish line.

3.44 Use figures for dimensions.

The form measured 6 by 8 inches.
The rug was designed to fit a room measuring 14' x 19'.

3.45 Use figures for scientific measurements of distances, length, area, volume, pressure, etc. In scientific work no periods appear after abbreviations.

16 grams	230 volts
161 psi	46 meters
161 mi	2,617 cm

3.46 Use figures for quantities given in pints, quarts, bushels, etc.

The plants produced 147 quarts of the chemical each hour.
The recipe called for 2 pints of milk and 3 quarts of ice cream.

3.47 Use figures for weights.

The elephant weighed 4,667 pounds; the baby raccoon weighed only
    6 ounces.

3.48 Use figures for temperatures, with the degree symbol °. To express temperatures in Celsius, use the symbol °C.

The temperature was 97° at noon today.
The temperature that morning was −3°C.

ROMAN NUMERALS

3.49 Roman numerals are frequently used to express volume and unit references in published materials. The general rule is that a letter before one of greater value subtracts from the value of the larger number; a letter after one of greater value adds to the value.

1	I	13	XIII
2	II	14	XIV
3	III	15	XV
4	IV	16	XVI
5	V	17	XVII
6	VI	18	XVIII
7	VII	19	XIX
8	VIII	20	XX
9	IX	30	XXX
10	X	40	XL
11	XI	50	L
12	XII	60	LX

3.50

70	LXX		600	DC
80	LXXX		700	DCC
90	XC		800	DCCC
100	C		900	CM
200	CC		1,000	M
300	CCC		2,000	MM
400	CD		3,000	MMM
500	D		5,000	$\overline{V}$

SCORES AND VOTES

3.50 Use figures for scores of any kind and for results of elections.

The Crimson Flyers won by a score of 98–89.
Hunt won the tennis match 6–4, 6–7, 6–2.
A total of 69,500 votes were cast—30,495 for Jones and 39,005 for Wilson.

SYMBOLS

3.51 The following symbols are often used with expressions of numbers. They appear on most typewriter keyboards, but can be made using a combination of keys.

addition	+		exponent	8^2
ampersand (and)	&		feet, minutes	'
asterisk	*		inches, seconds	"
at or each	@		minus	−
brackets	[ ]		multiplication	x OR ·
cent(s)	¢		number or pound	#
degree	°		paragraph	¶
dollar(s)	$		parentheses	( )
division	÷		per	/
English pound	£		percent	%
equals	=		ratio	:

Self-Check Exercise

In the sentences below, circle the proper expression of the number.

1. We purchased (47, forty-seven) typewriters for the new office.
2. Mr. Joplin had 318 sales last month; Ms. Wilson, 43; and Miss Jones, (10, ten).
3. (27, Twenty-seven) people were hired for the new department.
4. The secretary asked the mail clerk for (13, thirteen) eight-cent stamps.
5. We ordered the desks on (May 13, May thirteen).
6. The meeting was to be held no later than (10, ten) o'clock; the results of the election were to be announced precisely at (four-thirty, 4:30).
7. The office is located at (5th, Fifth) and Elm Streets.
8. We purchased the copier for ($380, $380.00, three hundred eighty dollars).
9. Elaine said she would retire at about (65, sixty-five); she is now (forty-eight years, three months; 48 years, 3 months) old.
10. The reprographics room measured (10 × 15, ten by fifteen) feet.
11. Each typist will do (1/3, one-third, one third) of the work.
12. More than (20%, twenty percent) of the work had to be redone.
13. The (90th, Ninetieth) Congress enacted important legislation affecting education.
14. Soon after moving, they joined the (1st, First) Methodist Church.
15. Refer to page (eleven, 11) for the correct answer.
16. In the recent election, Harry Jones received over (thirty thousand, 30,000) votes.
17. Our trip took us over Interstate (Twenty, 20).
18. The office is located at (1, One) Beacon Street.
19. The pharmacist measured (16, sixteen) grams of the substance for the prescription.
20. For every dollar in the budget, (65, sixty-five) cents goes for salaries.

Check your answers in the back of the book.

4 Abbreviations

IN GENERAL, avoid most abbreviations because of the possibility of misunderstanding. However, abbreviations may be acceptable when traditionally used, when called for in technical writing, or when necessary because of spacing problems.

In deciding whether or not to abbreviate, it is generally wise to follow what has been the custom, what is needed to maintain clarity, and what is needed to maintain the degree of formality required. Abbreviations should generally not be used for ordinary words in business letters.

The trend appears to be away from the use of periods with abbreviations. Where they have traditionally appeared, periods have been left in the examples that follow. Whatever you do, be consistent!

ACADEMIC DEGREES

4.1 Abbreviate academic degrees if they follow full names.

Wilma R. Judd, Ph.D.   Myron Frank Cohen, M.A.

4.2 A list of common abbreviations for academic degrees follows.

A.A.	Associate of Arts
B.A. OR A.B.	Bachelor of Arts
B.B.A.	Bachelor of Business Administration
B.C.E.	Bachelor of Civil (or Chemical) Engineering
B.D.	Bachelor of Divinity
B.L.S.	Bachelor of Library Sciences
B.S.	Bachelor of Science
D.B.A.	Doctor of Business Administration
D.D.	Doctor of Divinity
D.D.S.	Doctor of Dental Surgery (or Science)
Ed.D.	Doctor of Education
Ed.S.	Doctor of Science
J.D.	Doctor of Jurisprudence (Law)
L.H.D.	Doctor of Humanities
Litt.D.	Doctor of Letters
LL.B.	Bachelor of Laws
LL.D.	Doctor of Laws
M.A.	Master of Arts

M.B.A.	Master of Business Administration
M.D.	Doctor of Medicine
M.Ed.	Master of Education
M.S.	Master of Science
Ph.D.	Doctor of Philosophy
Th.D.	Doctor of Theology

ADDRESSES AND GEOGRAPHICAL TERMS

4.3 The following terms are commonly abbreviated in addresses.

Ave.	Avenue	Pkwy.	Parkway
Bldg.	Building	Pl.	Place
Blvd.	Boulevard	Rd.	Road
Ct.	Court	Sq.	Square
Dr.	Drive	St.	Street
La. OR Ln.	Lane	Terr.	Terrace

4.4 When they stand alone, always spell out names of countries and their states, territories, and possessions.

4.5 The following table contains the standard and two-letter abbreviations (used with ZIP Codes) for states, districts, territories, and possessions of the United States. (The following states do not have standard abbreviations: Alaska, Hawaii, Idaho, Iowa, Maine, Ohio, and Utah.)

State	Standard Abbreviation	Two-letter Abbreviation
Alabama	Ala.	AL
Alaska		AK
Arizona	Ariz.	AZ
Arkansas	Ark.	AR
California	Calif.	CA
Colorado	Colo.	CO
Connecticut	Conn.	CT
Delaware	Del.	DE
Florida	Fla.	FL
Georgia	Ga.	GA
Hawaii		HI
Idaho		ID
Illinois	Ill.	IL
Indiana	Ind.	IN
Iowa		IA
Kansas	Kans.	KS
Kentucky	Ky.	KY
Louisiana	La.	LA

State	Standard Abbreviation	Two-letter Abbreviation
Maine		ME
Maryland	Md.	MD
Massachusetts	Mass.	MA
Michigan	Mich.	MI
Minnesota	Minn.	MN
Mississippi	Miss.	MS
Missouri	Mo.	MO
Montana	Mont.	MT
Nebraska	Nebr.	NE
Nevada	Nev.	NV
New Hampshire	N.H.	NH
New Jersey	N.J.	NJ
New Mexico	N. Mex.	NM
New York	N.Y.	NY
North Carolina	N.C.	NC
North Dakota	N. Dak.	ND
Ohio		OH
Oklahoma	Okla.	OK
Oregon	Oreg.	OR
Pennsylvania	Pa.	PA
Rhode Island	R.I.	RI
South Carolina	S.C.	SC
South Dakota	S. Dak.	SD
Tennessee	Tenn.	TN
Texas	Tex.	TX
Utah		UT
Vermont	Vt.	VT
Virginia	Va.	VA
Washington	Wash.	WA
West Virginia	W.Va.	WV
Wisconsin	Wis.	WI
Wyoming	Wyo.	WY

Districts, Territories, and Possessions of the United States

District of Columbia	D.C.	DC
Guam	Guam	GU
Puerto Rico	P.R.	PR
Virgin Islands	V.I.	VI

4.6 The following list includes the standard and two-letter abbreviations for Canadian provinces.

Province	Standard Abbreviation	Two-letter Abbreviation
Alberta	Alta.	AB
British Columbia	B.C.	BC
Labrador	Lab.	LB
Manitoba	Man.	MB
New Brunswick	N.B.	NB
Newfoundland	Newf./Nfld.	NF
Northwest Territories	N.W.T.	NT
Nova Scotia	N.S.	NS
Ontario	Ont.	ON
Prince Edward Island	P.E.I.	PE
Quebec	Que.	PQ
Saskatchewan	Sask.	SK
Yukon Territory	Y.T.	YT

COMPANY NAMES

4.7 The following abbreviations are often used as part of company names.

Bro.	Brother	Corp.	Corporation
Bros.	Brothers	Inc.	Incorporated
Co.	Company	Ltd.	Limited

COMPASS POINTS

4.8 When abbreviations of compass points are required, use the following.

N	North	NW	Northwest
S	South	SW	Southwest
E	East	NNE	North by Northeast
W	West	SSE	South by Southeast
NE	Northeast	NNW	North by Northwest
SE	Southeast	SSW	South by Southwest

COMPUTER TERMINOLOGY

4.9 The following are common computer abbreviations.

ADP	automatic data processing
ALGOL	Algorithmic Oriented Language
ASCII-8	American Standard Code for Information Interchange-8
BASIC	Beginner's All-purpose Symbolic Instruction Code

BCD	binary-coded decimal
COBOL	Common Business-Oriented Language
COM	computer-output microfilm (or microfiche)
CPU	central processing unit
CRT	cathode-ray tube
DASD	direct-access storage device
DSCB	data set control block
DSL	data set label
EBCDIC	Extended Binary-Coded Decimal Interchange Code
ECB	event control block
EDP	electronic data processing
EOF	end of file
ESD	external symbol dictionary
FORTRAN	Formula Translation
IDP	integrated data processing
I/O	input/output
IPL	initial program loading
MICR	magnetic ink character recognition
OCR	optical character recognition
OEM	original equipment manufacturer
OP code	operation code
QCB	queue control block

DATES AND TIMES

4.10 In text, spell out names of months and days of the week. They may be abbreviated, however, in tables and footnotes. When it is necessary, use the following.

Months of the Year

Jan.	January	July	July
Feb.	February	Aug.	August
Mar.	March	Sept.	September
Apr.	April	Oct.	October
May	May	Nov.	November
June	June	Dec.	December

Days of the Week

Sun.	Sunday	Thurs.	Thursday
Mon.	Monday	Fri.	Friday
Tues.	Tuesday	Sat.	Saturday
Wed.	Wednesday		

4.11 Abbreviate time periods of the day as follows.

    a.m. before noon (*ante meridiem*)
    p.m. after noon (*post meridiem*)

4.12 The time zones in the United States may be abbreviated as follows.

    CST Central Standard Time   MST Mountain Standard Time
    DST Daylight Saving Time   PST Pacific Standard Time
    EST Eastern Standard Time

4.13 Other abbreviations associated with time are as follows.

    A.D. *anno Domini* (in the year   min. minute
                of our Lord)   mo. month
    B.C. before Christ   sec. second
    d. day   yr. year
    hr. hour

GOVERNMENT AGENCIES

4.14 The following abbreviations are often used for well-known government agencies.

AEC	Atomic Energy Commission
CAA	Civil Aeronautics Agency
CAB	Civil Aeronautics Board
CIA	Central Intelligence Agency
CSC	Civil Service Commission
FBI	Federal Bureau of Investigation
FCC	Federal Communications Commission
FDA	Federal Drug Administration
FDIC	Federal Deposit Insurance Corporation
FHA	Federal Housing Administration
FICA	Federal Insurance Contributions Act
FPC	Federal Power Commission
FRB	Federal Reserve Bank (or Board)
FRS	Federal Reserve System
FSLIC	Federal Savings and Loan Insurance Corporation
FTC	Federal Trade Commission
HEW	Health, Education, and Welfare (Department of)
HUD	Housing and Urban Development
ICC	Interstate Commerce Commission
IRS	Internal Revenue Service
NASA	National Aeronautics and Space Administration
NBS	National Bureau of Standards
NCIC	National Crime Information Center

4.15

NLRB   National Labor Relations Board
NSC   National Security Council
PHA   Public Housing Administration
ROTC   Reserve Officers' Training Corps
SBA   Small Business Administration
SEC   Securities and Exchange Commission
SSA   Social Security Administration
SSS   Selective Service System
TVA   Tennessee Valley Authority
USA   United States Army
USAF   United States Air Force
USCG   United States Coast Guard
USIA   United States Information Agency
USMC   United States Marine Corps
USN   United States Navy
VA   Veterans' Administration

MEASUREMENT UNITS

4.15 The following abbreviations generally represent units of measure in the English system.

Length

in.	inch	rd.	rod (5½ yd.)
ft.	foot (12 in.)	mi.	mile (5,280 ft.)
yd.	yard (3 ft.)		

Area

sq. in.	square inch	sq. rd.	square rod
sq. ft.	square foot (144 sq. in.)		(30¼ sq. yd.)
		A.	acre (4,840 sq. yd.)
sq. yd.	square yard (9 sq. ft.)	sq. mi.	square mile (640 A.)

Volume

cu. in.	cubic inch	cu. yd.	cubic yard (27 cu. ft.)
cu. ft.	cubic foot (1,728 cu. in.)		

Weight

gr.	grain	lb.	pound (16 oz.)
dr.	dram (27.344 gr.)	cwt.	hundredweight (100 lb.)
oz.	ounce (16 dr.)		
		t.	ton (2,000 lb.)

Dry Measure

pt.	pint	pk.	peck (8 qt.)
qt.	quart (2 pt.)	bu.	bushel (4 pk.)

Liquid Measure

fl. oz.	fluid ounce	gal.	gallon (4 qt.)
pt.	pint (16 fl. oz.)	bbl.	barrel (31.5 gal.)
qt.	quart (2 pt.)		

4.16 The following list shows the metric equivalents of various English measurements.

1 in.	= 25.4 mm; 2.54 cm	1 pt.	= 0.47 ℓ
1 ft.	= 0.305 m	1 qt.	= 0.95 ℓ
1 yd.	= 0.91 m	1 gal.	= 3.79 ℓ
1 mi.	= 1.61 km		
		1 oz.	= 28.35 g
1 sq. in.	= 6.5 cm²	1 lb.	= 0.45 kg
1 sq. ft.	= 0.09 m²	1 t.	= 1,000 kg
1 sq. yd.	= 0.8 m²		
1 A.	= 4,047 m²		
1 cu in.	= 16.4 cm³		
1 cu. ft.	= 0.03 m³		
1 cu. yd.	= 0.8 m³		

METRIC MEASUREMENT

4.17 The following abbreviations are commonly used with metric measures.

Length

mm	millimeter	dam	decameter (10 m)
cm	centimeter (10 mm)	hm	hectometer (10 dam)
dm	decimeter (10 cm)	km	kilometer (10 hm)
m	meter (10 dm)		

Area

mm²	square millimeter	dam²	square decameter (100 m²)
cm²	square centimeter (100 mm²)	hm²	square hectometer (100 dam²)
dm²	square decimeter (100 cm²)	km²	square kilometer (100 hm²)
m²	square meter (100 dm²)		

4.18

Volume

mm³	cubic millimeter	dam³	cubic decameter
cm³	cubic centimeter		(1,000 m³)
	(1,000 mm³)	hm³	cubic hectometer
dm³	cubic decimeter		(1,000 dam³)
	(1,000 cm³)	km³	cubic kilometer
m³	cubic meter (1,000 dm³)		(1,000 hm³)

Weight

mg	milligram	dag	decagram (10 g)
cg	centigram (10 mg)	hg	hectogram (10 dag)
dg	decigram (10 cg)	kg	kilogram (10 hg)
g	gram (10 dg)		

Capacity

ml	milliliter	dal	decaliter (10 ℓ)
cl	centiliter (10 ml)	hl	hectoliter (10 dal)
dl	deciliter (10 cl)	kl	kiloliter (10 hl)
ℓ	liter (10 cl)		

4.18 The following list shows the English equilvalents of various metric quantities.

1 mm	=	0.04 in.		1 ml	=	0.034 oz.
1 cm	=	0.4 in.		1 cl	=	0.34 oz.
1 m	=	39.37 in.		1 ℓ	=	2.1 pt.; 1.06 qt.;
1 km	=	0.6 mi.				0.26 gal.
1 cm²	=	0.16 sq. in.		1 g	=	0.035 oz.
1 m²	=	10.8 sq. ft.;		1 kg	=	2.2 lb.
		1.2 sq. yd.				
1 cm³	=	0.06 cu. in.				
1 m³	=	35.3 cu. ft.;				
		1.3 cu. yd.				

NAMES

4.19 As a rule, do not abbreviate the given names of individuals.

William (not Wm.) Randolph   Elizabeth (not Eliz.) Browning

4.20 Signatures should be shown as written by the person.

Geo. Scott (signature)   Benj. Ryan (signature)

4.21 Use no periods when referring to notable persons by initials only.

LBJ (Lyndon Baines Johnson)   FDR (Franklin Delano Roosevelt)

ORGANIZATIONS

4.22 The following abbreviations are often used for well-known organizations.

AAA	American Automobile Association
ABA	American Bankers Association; American Bar Association
ABC	American Broadcasting Company
AFL-CIO	American Federation of Labor-Congress of Industrial Organizations
AIB	American Institute of Banking
AMA	American Medical Association
AMS	American Management Society
AP	Associated Press
ARMA	Association of Records Managers and Administrators
BBB	Better Business Bureau
BBC	British Broadcasting Corporation
CBS	Columbia Broadcasting System
GOP	"Grand Old Party" (Republican)
IBM	International Business Machines
MBS	Mutual Broadcasting System
NAACP	National Association for the Advancement of Colored People
NAM	National Association of Manufacturers
NATO	North Atlantic Treaty Organization
NBC	National Broadcasting Company
NCR	National Cash Register
NEA	National Education Association
OPEC	Organization of Petroleum Exporting Countries
PBS	Public Broadcasting System
PTA	Parent-Teachers Association
RCA	Radio Corporation of America
SPCA	Society for the Prevention of Cruelty to Animals
UN	United Nations
UNESCO	United Nations Educational, Scientific, and Cultural Organization
UNICEF	United Nations International Children's Emergency Fund
UPI	United Press International
WHO	World Health Organization
YMCA	Young Men's Christian Association
YWCA	Young Women's Christian Association

4.23 It is generally acceptable practice to spell out a company or organization name when first used, then abbreviate it in the remainder of the writing if the abbreviation is well known.

SCIENTIFIC TERMS

4.24 The following are common scientific abbreviations.

A	ampere	ft-lb	foot-pound
Å	angstrom unit	hp	horsepower
a.c. OR ac	alternating current	°K	degree Kelvin
AM	amplitude modulation	kW	kilowatt
at wt	atomic weight	m.p.	melting point
avdp.	avoirdupois	mph	miles per hour
bar.	barometer	neg.	negative
bp	boiling point	psi	pounds per square inch
Btu	British thermal unit	R	roentgen
°C	degree Celsius (centigrade)	r.p.m.	revolutions per minute
cal	calorie	sp gr	specific gravity
cc	cubic centimeter	std.	standard
d.c. OR dc	direct current	T	temperature
dB	decibel	V	volt
deg.	degree	W	watt
°F	degree Fahrenheit	wt	weight
FM	frequency modulation		

TITLES

4.25 Do not abbreviate civil, military, or religious titles preceding surnames (last names).

General Wyland (not Gen. Wyland)
Senator O'Malley (not Sen. O'Malley)
Reverend Wheatley (not Rev. Wheatley)

4.26 Civil, military, or religious titles that precede full names may be abbreviated.

Gen. Howard T. Wyland   Sen. Marie Gaston O'Malley
Rev. Marvin Wheatley

4.27 Always abbreviate social titles.

Mr.	Mister	M.	Monsieur
Mrs.	Mistress	Mme.	Madame
Ms.	Miss or Mrs.	Mlle.	Mademoiselle
Messrs.	Messieurs (plural of Mr.)		

4.28 Abbreviate seniority titles that follow full names.

Henry S. Trout, Jr.   William Harvey, Sr.

COMMON ABBREVIATIONS

4.29 The following is a list of common abbreviations not found in the preceding sections.

abbr.	abbreviation	ch. OR chap.	chapter
abr.	abridged	c.i.f.	cost, insurance, and freight
acct.	account		
ad val. OR a.v.	*ad valorem* (in proportion to the value)	c.l.	carload
		c/o	in care of
amt.	amount	COD	collect (or cash) on delivery
anon.	anonymous	cont.	continued
ans.	answer	CPA	certified public accountant
apt.	apartment		
assn.	association	CPS	certified professional secretary
asst.	assistant		
Att. OR Attn.	attention		
atty.	attorney	cr.	credit, creditor
bal.	balance	cust.	customer
B/F	brought forward	dept.	department
bk.	book	disc.	discount
B/L	bill of lading	dist.	district
bx.	box	div.	dividend, division, divisor
C	one hundred		
cap.	capital, capitalize	doz.	dozen
		dr.	debit
cat.	catalogue	ea.	each
cc	carbon copy	ed.	edition
C/D	certificate of deposit	e.g.	*exempli gratia* (for example)
cf	confer, compare	enc.	enclosure

4.29

e.o.m.	end of month
Esq.	Esquire
est.	estimated
et al.	*et alii* (and others)
etc.	*et cetera* (and so forth)
ex.	example
fed.	federal
ff.	and the following pages
FIFO	first in, first out
fig.	figure
f.o.b.	free on board
frt.	freight
fwd.	forward
govt.	government
hq.	headquarters
ibid.	*ibidem* (in the same place)
i.e.	*id est* (that is)
incl.	inclusive
int.	interest
IOU	I owe you
IQ	intelligence quotient
ital.	italic
jour.	journal
J.P.	justice of the peace
Jr.	junior
k	carat
lat.	latitude
L/C	letter of credit
lc	lowercase
LIFO	last in, first out
loc. cit.	*loco citato* (in the place cited)
long.	longitude
L.S.	*locus sigilli* (in the place of the seal)
max.	maximum
mdse.	merchandise
memo	memorandum
mfg.	manufacturing
mgr.	manager
min.	minimum
misc.	miscellaneous
mkt.	market
n/30	net in 30 days
N.B.	*nota bene* (note well)
no.	number
op. cit.	*opere citato* (in the work cited)
orig.	original
p.	page
PBX	Private Branch Exchange
pd.	paid
P.O.	post office
pp.	pages
pr.	pair
P.S.	postscript
qr.	quarter
re.	regarding
recd.	received
ref.	reference
Rep.	Representative, Republican
rm.	ream
R.N.	registered nurse
rom.	roman (type)
RR	railroad
R.R.	rural route
r.s.v.p.	respond, if you please
rte.	route
Ry.	railway
Sr.	senior
S.R.O.	standing room only
St.	saint
supt.	superintendent
treas.	treasurer

TV	television	VHF	very high frequency
TWX	teletypewriter exchange	VIP	very important person
UFO	unidentified flying object	vol.	volume
UHF	ultrahigh frequency	vs.	versus
univ.	university	wt.	weight
UPC	Universal Product Code	ZIP	Zone Improvement Plan

Self-Check Exercise

Indicate whether the following abbreviations (or their definitions) are correctly represented by writing yes or no in the space provided.

_____ 1. Gen. Douglas MacArthur

_____ 2. Col. Winslow

_____ 3. Mister Jonathon Hensley

_____ 4. Marvin C. Stout, Jr.

_____ 5. B.A. (Bachelor of Arts)

_____ 6. D.L. (Doctor of Laws)

_____ 7. B.Sc. (Bachelor of Science)

_____ 8. M.B.A. (Master of Business Administration

_____ 9. M.Arts (Master of Arts)

_____ 10. M.S. (Master of Science)

_____ 11. E.D. (Doctor of Education)

_____ 12. Ph.D. (Doctor of Philosophy)

_____ 13. AMA (American Medical Association)

_____ 14. IBM (International Business Machines)

_____ 15. CIA (Central Intelligence Association)

_____ 16. FDIC (Federal Deposit Insurance Corporation)

_____ 17. SXC (Securities and Exchange Commission)

_____ 18. Ap. (April)

_____ 19. Sept. (September)

_____ 20. Mn. (Monday)

_____ 21. Ths. (Thursday)

_____ 22. a.m. (*ante meridiem;* before noon)

_____ 23. B.C. (before Christ)

_____ 24. vs. (versus)

_____ 25. d. (day)

_____ 26. in. (inch)

_____ 27. sq. ft. (square foot)

_____ 28. hwt. (hundredweight)

_____ 29. qt. (quart)

_____ 30. bl. (barrel)

_____ 31. km (kilometer)

_____ 32. mt (meter)

_____ 33. cg (centigram)

_____ 34. g (gram)

_____ 35. Ce (Celsius)

_____ 36. mph (miles per hour)

_____ 37. CRT (cathode-ray tube)

_____ 38. MICR (magnetic ink character recognition)

_____ 39. OCR (optical code recognition)

_____ 40. Ark. and AR (Arkansas)

_____ 41. Cali. and CA (California)

_____ 42. Hawaii and HI (Hawaii)

_____ 43. Io. and IA (Iowa)

_____ 44. Kans. and KS (Kansas)

_____ 45. Ma. and MC (Massachusetts)

_____ 46. Mich. and MI (Michigan)

_____ 47. Mo. and MS (Missouri)

_____ 48. Tx. and TE (Texas)

_____ 49. Wash. and WA (Washington)

_____ 50. B/F (brought forward)

_____ 51. c.i.f. (cost, installation, and freight)

_____ 52. dept. (department)

_____ 53. mdse. (merchandise)

_____ 54. dr. (debit)

_____ 55. e.o.m. (end of month)

_____ 56. f.o.b. (freight on board)

_____ 57. LIFO (last in, first out)

_____ 58. n/30 (net in 30 days)

_____ 59. CPS (certified professional secretary)

_____ 60. e.g. (for example)

Check your answers in the back of the book.

5 Grammar

TO BE ABLE to communicate effectively, you must possess a mastery of the tools of communication. A knowledge of grammar, one of the tools of communication, will permit you to write and speak more effectively.

ADJECTIVES

5.1 An *adjective* is a word that modifies a noun or a pronoun by telling which one, what kind, or how many.

> The employee in the *front* row complained about the *company* cafeteria.
> The *happy* executive signed the contract.
> There were *numerous* complaints about the delay in completing the work.
> They were *busy* on Friday.

5.2 A *proper adjective* is an adjective derived from a proper noun or a proper noun used as an adjective. A proper adjective is always capitalized.

> He assisted the manager in preparing for the *European* trip.
> The secretary laid the *Boston* papers on the desk.

5.3 A *compound adjective* consists of two or more words combined to form a single descriptive adjective. It is generally hyphenated only if it immediately precedes the noun it modifies.

> The report indicated that the *hard-to-find* items caused difficulty.
> The report indicated that the items causing difficulty were *hard to find*.

5.4 Adjectives are often used to compare two or more persons or things. To do this, adjectives have different forms, or *degrees*. The three degrees of comparison are the positive, the comparative, and the superlative.

5.5 The *positive form* is used when there is no comparison being made. The adjective modifies only one person or thing.

> Ms. Wilson is a *fast* typist.

5.6 The *comparative degree* is used to compare two persons or things. Comparative degree is usually formed by adding *-er* to the positive form.

Ms. Wilson is a *faster* typist than Mr. Long.

To form the comparative degree of most adjectives having more than two syllables and most adjectives that end in *-ful* or *-less,* add the word "more" or "less" to the positive form.

Charlene is a *more accurate* typist than Donna.
Paul is *less helpful* than Jo.

5.7 The *superlative degree* is used to compare three or more persons or things. Superlative degree is usually formed by adding *-est* to the positive form.

Ms. Wilson is the *fastest* typist of the three.

To form the superlative degree of most adjectives that have more than two syllables and most adjectives that end in *-ful* or *-less,* add the word "most" or "least" to the positive form.

Charlene is the *most accurate* typist in the department.
Harriett is the *least helpful* of all the supervisors in the office.

5.8 Some adjectives show the comparative and superlative degrees in irregular ways.

Positive	Comparative	Superlative
bad	worse	worst
good	better	best
many	more	most

ADVERBS

5.9 An *adverb* is a word that modifies a verb, an adjective, or another adverb. Adverbs tell when, where, how, and how much. Many adverbs are formed by adding the suffix *-ly* to an adjective.

Miss Langley completed the letter *immediately.*
The executive looked *down* at the printout before quoting the figure.
The supervisor *quickly* demonstrated how to operate the machine.
The supervisor appreciates *very much* the work of Janice.

5.10 Adverbs, like adjectives, can be used to compare two or more things. They too have three degrees: positive, comparative, and superlative.

5.11 The *positive form* is used when no comparison is being made.

John works *hard.*

5.12 The *comparative degree* is used when two things or persons are being compared. Comparative degree is formed by adding *-er* to the positive form or by using the word "more" or "less" with the positive form.

John works *harder* than Frank.
Of the two, Jan does her work *more neatly.*

5.13 The *superlative degree* is used when comparing more than two things or people. Superlative degree is formed by adding *-est* to the positive form or by using the word "most" or "least" with the positive form.

Of the three employees, Tony works *hardest.*
Jan's work was the *most neatly* done.

CONJUNCTIONS

5.14 A *conjunction* is a word that joins words, phrases, or clauses. There are three types of conjunctions: coordinating, correlating, and subordinating.

5.15 A *coordinating conjunction* joins elements of equal rank. The most commonly used coordinating conjunctions are *and, but,* and *or.*

The workers *and* the supervisors in the warehouse *and* the office met on Friday.
The typist prepared the report on time, *but* it was not delivered promptly.
You must decide whether typing the report *or* proofreading the report will be the most important task.

5.16 *Correlating conjunctions* are coordinating conjunctions used in pairs to connect two elements of equal value. Commonly used correlating conjunctions are:

either/or	both/and
neither/nor	not only/but also
whether/or	

Richard *not only* typed the report, *but also* proofread it carefully.
Either he will arrange the conference, *or* I will do it.

5.17 A *subordinating conjunction* joins dependent clauses to independent clauses. Commonly used subordinating conjunctions are:

after	in order that
although	since
as	so that
as if	than
as soon as	that
as though	though
because	unless
before	until
for	when
if	where
inasmuch as	wherever
in case	while

Although he had completed the report, Kevin did not present it to the committee.

INTERJECTIONS

5.18 An *interjection* is a word that expresses very strong feelings or sudden reactions. An exclamation point follows an interjection.

Wow! The new machine really turns out the work.
Stop! The paper is upside-down in the machine.

NOUNS

5.19 A *noun* is a word that names a person, place, thing, or idea. Nouns can be classified according to the kinds of things they name.

5.20 A *common noun* identifies a person, place, thing, or idea in a general class.

In the *office, people* work hard to prepare *reports* on *time.*

5.21 A *proper noun* identifies a particular person, place, or thing. A proper noun is always capitalized.

John Riley works in *New York City* for the *Central Publishing Company.*

5.22 A *collective noun* refers to groups of people, animals, and things.

audience	company
band	committee
class	council
club	crew

crowd	jury
faculty	pack
family	squad
flock	staff
group	team
herd	troop

5.23 If a collective noun refers to the group acting as one unit, use a singular verb.

The class takes its first examination on Monday.
The committee votes on every issue that comes before it.

5.24 If a collective noun refers to a group in which the members act independently, use a plural verb.

The *class have been required* to submit reports frequently.
The *committee were not impressed* by the reports.

5.25 A *concrete noun* refers to something that can be seen directly.

She is my *friend*.

5.26 An *abstract noun* refers to a concept or idea, something that can be thought about but cannot be seen directly.

Nothing can end our *friendship*.

PREPOSITIONS

5.27 A *preposition* is a word that is used to join a noun or a pronoun to another part of the sentence. Commonly used prepositions include:

about	from
above	in
after	into
against	of
among	on
around	onto
at	over
before	through
below	to
beside	under
between	until
by	upon
except	with
for	within

The manager *of* the department talked *with* the supervisors *about* the plan.
She tucked the folder *in* the briefcase *under* the stack *of* catalogues.

5.28 A *prepositional phrase* is a group of words consisting of the preposition, modifier, and a noun or pronoun.

On the day he left, Mr. Masters placed the report *in the mail.*
Because *of his absence*, the checks lay unsigned *on the desk.*

5.29 If a prepositional phrase modifies a noun or pronoun, it is called an *adjective phrase.*

The typist *with the long blonde hair* is Miss Smith. (modifies *typist*)

5.30 If a prepositional phrase modifies an adjective, adverb, or verb, it is called an *adverbial phrase.*

She was slow *in her work.* (modifies *slow*)
The receptionist's desk was placed *behind the partition.* (modifies *was placed*)
He works quickly and accurately *in every task.* (modifies *quickly* and *accurately*)

PRONOUNS

5.31 A *pronoun* is a word used to replace or refer to a noun.

5.32 *Personal pronouns* refer to a particular person or thing. Personal pronouns are usually referred to in terms of *person* (first, second, or third), *number* (singular or plural), *gender* (masculine, feminine, or neuter), and *case* (nominative, objective, or possessive).

Person

5.33 By changing their form, personal pronouns can indicate whether the pronoun refers to the speaker (first person), to the speaker's audience (second person), or to everyone else (third person). The following chart indicates the pronouns that are used with first, second, and third person.

Person	Singular	Plural
First	I, me, my, mine	we, us, our, ours
Second	you, your, yours	you, your, yours
Third	he, she, it, him, her, his, hers, its	they, them, their, theirs

Number

5.34 Most personal pronouns have singular or plural form. *Singular* form indicates only one person or thing. *Plural* form indicates two or more people or things. The pronoun *you*, however, is used for both singular and plural form.

Jane gave the keys to *me*.
Three of *us* received *our* degrees.
I told *you* about *your* friend.
She told the class, "*You* must work harder."

Gender

5.35 Only third person personal pronouns can be classified by gender. The *masculine* pronouns are *he, his,* and *him*. The *feminine* pronouns are *she, hers,* and *her*. *It* is of *neuter* gender and refers to things that are neither masculine nor feminine.

All other personal pronouns (*I, you, your, our, ours, they, their,* and *them*) are referred to as *common gender* pronouns since they can be either masculine or feminine.

Case

5.36 Depending on their use in sentences, pronouns can be in the nominative, objective, or possessive case.

5.37 The personal pronouns *I, he, she, we,* and *they* are in the *nominative case* and are used as subjects or predicate nominatives of sentences.

Working alone, *he* completed the task by midnight. (subject)
They directed the activities of the program. (subject)
The developer of the artwork for the project was *she*. (predicate nominative)

5.38 The personal pronouns *me, him, her, us,* and *them* are in the *objective case* and are used as the objects of verbs and prepositions.

Dr. Roberts took *them* on a tour of the hospital. (object of verb *took*)
While pointing out the difficulties, Ms. Wong agrees with *us* in principle. (object of preposition *with*)

5.39 The personal pronouns *my, mine, your, yours, his, hers, its, our, ours, their,* and *theirs* are in the *possessive case* and are used to show ownership.

The word processing supervisors gave *their* report on Monday. (shows
   possession of *report*)

5.40 The personal pronouns *you* and *it* can be in either nominative case or
objective case, depending on how they are used in the sentence.

You must be at work by nine o'clock. (subject)
It was the receptionist who answered the phone. (subject)
After typing the memo, the secretary gave *it* to the manager. (object of
   verb *gave*)
Paul is going to the meeting with *you*. (object of preposition *with*)

Agreement

5.41 The noun to which the pronoun refers is known as its *antecedent*.
Personal pronouns must agree with their antecedents in number and
gender.

Miss Ralston removed the cover from *her* typewriter. (The pronoun *her*
   refers to its antecedent *Miss Ralston*, which is singular in number
   and feminine in gender.)
The secretaries completed *their* work in record time. (The plural pronoun *their* refers to its antecedent *secretaries*, which is also plural.)
The mail cart lost *its* wheel as William turned the corner sharply. (The
   singular pronoun *its* refers to its antecedent *cart*, which is singular
   in number and neuter in gender.)

5.42 A plural pronoun must be used when referring to two or more antecedents joined by the word "and."

Ms. Tillson and *Mr. White* agreed to present *their* reports together.

5.43 When two business titles refer to the same person, use a singular
pronoun.

The *comptroller and secretary* gave *her* recommendations to the
   board. (The comptroller and secretary are the same person.)

5.44 When two business titles refer to two different people, use a plural
pronoun.

The *vice president* and the *treasurer* indicated *they* wanted more time
   to study the proposal. (The vice president and the treasurer are two
   different people.)

The word "the" used before *both* titles is usually an indication of two
different people.

5.45 When adjectives such as *each, every, many, a,* and *an* are used with two or more antecedents joined by *and,* use a singular pronoun.

> *Every* supervisor, clerk, and manager was informed of *her* increased benefits.

5.46 Antecedents of common gender may be dealt with in a number of ways. A combination of masculine and feminine gender pronouns may be used.

> The *worker* will sign *his or her* name on the time card.

This, however, tends to become awkward when overused.
  Another approach is to use either a masculine or feminine pronoun depending on how the gender of the antecedent is perceived.

> The *librarian* stacked the books on *her* desk.
> The *construction worker* carried the beam on *his* back.

The traditional approach has been to use the singular masculine pronoun for all singular common gender antecedents.

> The *driver* pulled *his* car up to the gasoline pump.
> When a *student* signs the card, *he* will receive the book.

These last two approaches, however, tend to encourage sexual stereotyping and are neither desirable nor accurate.
  Perhaps the best alternative is to rewrite the sentence to eliminate the singular pronoun.

> In order to maintain *her* professional competency, a *nurse* must return to school on occasion.
> In order to maintain *their* professional competency, *nurses* must return to school on occasion.

Indefinite Pronouns

5.47 *Indefinite pronouns* do not refer to a specific person or thing. Indefinite pronouns such as *anyone, anything, somebody, someone, everybody, everyone,* and *everything* are generally used with singular pronouns.

> *Everybody* brought *his* copy of the brochure to the meeting.
> *Anyone* was allowed to apply for *her* vacation that month.

Interrogative Pronouns

5.48 *Interrogative pronouns* are used to ask questions and include *who,* *whom, whose, which,* and *what. Who* is always used as a subject or predicate nominative and is always in the nominative case.

Who is responsible for completing the statement? (subject)

Whom is always used as the object of a verb or preposition and is always in the objective case.

Whom did you recommend for the position? (object of *did recommend*)

Whose is used to show ownership and is always in the possessive case.

Whose suggestion was adopted at the meeting?

Which and *what* may be used as subjects or objects in sentences and may, therefore, be in the nominative or objective case.

Which is the better report?
What did the committee propose?

Relative Pronouns

5.49 *Relative pronouns* are used to join subordinate clauses to antecedents. The relative pronouns *who, whom,* and *whose* refer to people; *which* refers to animals and things; and *that* refers to people, animals, or things.

Randy Clark is the *manager who* will represent the office.
The *report, which* you referred to, has been duplicated.
The service manager removed the *copier that* was broken.

VERBS

5.50 A *verb* is a word that shows action, condition, or a state of being.

The mail clerk *threw* the letters into the basket.
Miss Hamilton *is* the manager of the Boston office.
It *appears* that the report is factual.

A verb may be only one word or may consist of more than one word. A *verb phrase* is the main verb plus one or more auxiliary, or helping, verbs. Common auxiliary verbs are: is, be, am, are, was, were, been, have, has, had, may, must, ought, can, might, could, would, should, shall, will, do, does, and did.

Bernice *can operate* the duplicating equipment.
Lyle *did prepare* the report.
They *must reserve* the conference room for the meeting.

The parts of a verb phrase are often separated by other words.

I *do* not *think* she read the book.

Principal Parts of Verbs

5.51 All verbs have three principal parts: the present, the past, and the
past participle. These parts are used to form the various tenses in
sentences.

Most verbs form the past and the past participle by adding *-d* or *-ed*
to the present form.

Present	Past	Past Participle
agree	agreed	agreed
call	called	called

Some verbs, however, are *irregular*. They usually form the past and
past participle by changing their spelling or by keeping the same
spelling for all parts.

5.52 The following list shows the principal parts of common irregular
verbs.

Present	Past	Past Participle
arise	arose	arisen
awake	awoke/awaked	awoke/awaked
be/am/is/are	was/were	been
become	became	become
begin	began	begun
bite	bit	bitten
blow	blew	blown
bring	brought	brought
build	built	built
buy	bought	bought
catch	caught	caught
choose	chose	chosen
come	came	come
cut	cut	cut
do	did	done
draw	drew	drawn
drink	drank	drunk
drive	drove	driven

Present	Past	Past Participle
eat	ate	eaten
fall	fell	fallen
feed	fed	fed
feel	felt	felt
fight	fought	fought
find	found	found
fly	flew	flown
forget	forgot	forgotten
freeze	froze	frozen
get	got	got/gotten
give	gave	given
go	went	gone
grow	grew	grown
hang (execute)	hanged	hanged
hang (suspend)	hung	hung
have	had	had
hide	hid	hidden
hold	held	held
hurt	hurt	hurt
keep	kept	kept
know	knew	known
lay	laid	laid
lead	led	led
leave	left	left
lend	lent	lent
lie	lay	lain
lose	lost	lost
make	made	made
meet	met	met
pay	paid	paid
ride	rode	ridden
ring	rang	rung
rise	rose	risen
run	ran	run
say	said	said
see	saw	seen
sell	sold	sold
shake	shook	shaken
shine	shone	shone
sing	sang	sung
sink	sank/sunk	sunk
sit	sat	sat
speak	spoke	spoken
spring	sprang	sprung
stand	stood	stood
steal	stole	stolen
strike	struck	struck/stricken
swear	swore	sworn
swim	swam	swum
swing	swung	swung
take	took	taken
tear	tore	torn

Present	Past	Past Participle
tell	told	told
throw	threw	thrown
wear	wore	worn
write	wrote	written

While there are some patterns in the ways these verbs form the past and the past participle, there are inconsistencies. It is probably best to memorize these verbs or consult a dictionary when you are in doubt.

Tense

5.53 The tense of a verb tells when an action happened or when something existed. Tense tells *time*. In the English language, there are six basic tenses: present, past, future, present perfect, past perfect, and future perfect.

5.54 The *present tense* indicates an action occurring now, an action regularly done, or something that is a general truth.

Paula *agrees* with the proposal.
John usually *walks* to work.
Earth *is* 93 million miles from the sun.

The present tense may also be used to show a future action when the time is specified.

The ship *sails* next Tuesday.

Use the present form of the verb for the present tense.

5.55 The *past tense* indicates an action or condition in the past.

Lynn *presented* the report last Wednesday.
The winter of 1978 *was* harsh.

Use the past form of the verb for the past tense.

5.56 The *future tense* indicates an action that has not yet occurred.

They *will give* their reports tomorrow.
I *shall come* with you to the meeting.

Use *shall* or *will* and the present form of the verb for the future tense.

5.57 The *present perfect tense* indicates an action that has been completed by the time the statement is made.

I *have purchased* my airplane ticket.
Baker *has completed* the report.

Use *has* or *have* and the past participle of the verb for the present perfect tense.

5.58 The *past perfect tense* indicates an action completed in the past before another action, also in the past.

They *had gone* to lunch by the time I arrived.

Use *had* and the past participle of the verb for the past perfect tense.

5.59 The *future perfect tense* indicates an action begun in the past that will be completed in the future.

Andrew *will have retired* by June 1.

Use *will have* or *shall have* and the past participle of the verb for the future perfect tense.

Voice

5.60 A verb is in *active voice* when the subject of the sentence directs the action.

Harriett *threw* the stack of papers into the wastebasket. (The subject is *Harriett;* the active verb, *threw.*)

Active verbs are generally preferred in most writing because they are more forceful and express more action.

5.61 A verb is in *passive voice* when the subject of the sentence receives the action.

The task *was completed* by John by the end of the day. (The subject is *task;* the passive verb, *was completed.*)

Agreement

5.62 Subjects and verbs must agree in person and number. Singular nouns that are subjects require singular verbs, which generally end in *s*.

A *student needs* time for homework each night.

Some singular subjects may be separated from the verb by plural modifiers; nevertheless, a singular verb is required.

Mr. Hansen, along with three assistants, *walks* through the plant every day at this time.
Miss Allison, in addition to many other supervisors, *agrees* with the policy.

5.63 Plural nouns that are subjects require plural verbs, which generally do not end in *s*.

Students need time for homework every night.
Paula and *Jane prepare* that report every week.

Gerunds

5.64 A *gerund* is a verb form that ends in *-ing* and is used as a noun. Gerunds can be subjects, objects, and predicate nominatives.

Running is a good way to stay in shape. (subject)
She objected to *smoking* in the hallway. (object of preposition *to*)
The biggest task is *typing*. (predicate nominative)

Nouns or pronouns used to modify gerunds should always be in the possessive case.

Jim's talking kept him in trouble with the instructor.
The supervisor alluded to *their* copying the forms.

Infinitives

5.65 An *infinitive* is a verb form that usually consists of *to* plus a verb.

She wanted *to go* to the office early.

Infinitives may be used as nouns, adjectives, or adverbs.
    It is generally better to avoid separating the parts of the infinitive with an intervening word.

We were asked *to* carefully *prepare* the report.
We were asked *to prepare* the report carefully.

Participles

5.66 A *participle* is a verb form used as an adjective to describe nouns and pronouns.

> *Reading* the report, Mrs. Martinez paused to reflect over its contents. (describes *Mrs. Martinez*)
> The person *typing* the report is Harry Jenssen. (describes *person*)

Lack of attention to correct placement of participles may result in confusion. Such errors are referred to as "dangling" participles. Participles, therefore, should be placed close to the words they describe.

> *Typing* with great speed, the report was completed by the secretary within an hour. (It appears that the report is typing with great speed!)
> *Typing* with great speed, the secretary completed the report within an hour.

Self-Check Exercise

SECTION I

In the sentences below, indicate the part of speech for each italicized word as follows:

adj (adjective)	int (interjection)	pro (pronoun)
adv (adverb)	n (noun)	v (verb)
conj (conjunction)	prep (preposition)	

Example: The *memorandum* *directed* *us* to complete the report *immediately*.

<small>above *memorandum*: n   above *directed*: v   above *us*: pro   above *immediately*: adv</small>

1. *Wow!* The *team easily* won the *championship* series.
2. *They* mailed the package *because* they *were told* to do so.
3. *In* all *my* years on the *job*, I *rarely* missed a day.
4. *Marilyn* is the *fastest* worker *on* the assembly line.
5. The *police led* the suspect *into* the *quiet* courtroom.

SECTION II

Circle the correct word from those given in parentheses.

1. John is the (faster, fastest) of the two; Marilyn is the (faster, fastest) of them all.
2. Mr. Williams, one of the owners, took (his, their) family with him to the convention.
3. An unexpected flurry of orders and a breakdown of the delivery truck (has, have) caused the shipments to be delayed.
4. Many customers, along with the developer of the product, (is, are) happy with their purchases.
5. The typist completed the jobs, covered the typewriter, and put away (his, their) supplies.
6. The copier, (who, which) we purchased, proved to be very efficient.
7. The team (practice, practices) every day at four o'clock.
8. (Who, Whom) did you say was responsible for the error?
9. It was (she, her) who answered the telephone.
10. Everybody must do (her, their) best to reach the quota.

Check your answers in the back of the book.

6 Word Division and Hyphenation

IN ORDER to make the right margin of typed copy fairly even, it is sometimes necessary to divide a word at the end of a line. Rules for word division were once strictly defined and closely followed. However, with the new emphasis on productivity and cost consciousness and with the advent of high-speed computer printing technology, some of the rules have been relaxed. There are still a few basic rules that should always be followed, and others that should be followed if at all possible.

WORD DIVISION

6.1 Divide a word only between syllables; never divide a one-syllable word, regardless of its length.

com-pound	fur-ther
fol-low-ing	leg-is-la-tion
rolled	strength
turned	tripped

Dictionaries are good sources of syllabication. However, the syllable breaks are not always acceptable for end-of-line breaks.

6.2 Never divide a word of five or fewer letters.

undo	NOT	un-do
refer	NOT	re-fer
never	NOT	nev-er
allow	NOT	al-low

6.3 If a word contains a single-letter syllable, divide the word after this syllable.

regu-late	NOT	reg-ulate
dedi-cate	NOT	ded-icate
monopo-lize	NOT	monop-olize

6.4 Divide a word ending in *-ily, -able, -ably, -acle, -icle, -ical,* and the like before these suffixes.

favor-ably	NOT	favora-bly
read-ily	NOT	readi-ly
reach-able	NOT	reacha-ble
man-acle	NOT	mana-cle
enjoy-able	NOT	enjoya-ble

6.5 Divide a word between two single-letter syllables that appear together.

continu-ation	NOT	contin-uation
gradu-ation	NOT	gradua-tion

6.6 Include two or more letters with the first part of a divided word and three or more with the last part.

aban-doned	NOT	a-bandoned
ideal-istic	NOT	i-dealistic
around	NOT	a-round
erased	NOT	e-rased
rever-ently	NOT	reverent-ly
adver-sity	NOT	adversi-ty

6.7 If a root word ends in a double consonant before a suffix is added, divide *after* the double consonant.

bill-ing	NOT	bil-ling
trespass-ing	NOT	trespas-sing
drill-ing	NOT	dril-ling

6.8 If the final letter in a root word is doubled before a suffix is added, divide between the doubled letters.

get-ting	NOT	gett-ing
sublet-ting	NOT	sublett-ing
refer-ring	NOT	referr-ing
ship-ping	NOT	shipp-ing

6.9 If at all possible, divide a compound word between the compound elements.

letter-head	NOT	let-terhead
basket-ball	NOT	bas-ketball
common-wealth	NOT	com-monwealth

6.10 If a compound word is hyphenated, divide at the point of the hyphen.

self-addressed	NOT	self-ad-dressed
self-improvement	NOT	self-im-provement

6.11 Divide dates, proper nouns, and addresses only if unavoidable. When they must be divided, divide at the point of greatest readability.

Dates

January 3, / 1980	NOT	January / 3, 1980

Proper nouns

Applegate	NOT	Apple-gate
Mr. John / Smith	NOT	Mr. / John Smith
Linda / Barnes, Ph.D.	NOT	Linda Barnes, / Ph.D.

Addresses

Chicago, / IL 60633	NOT	Chicago, IL / 60633

6.12 Avoid dividing figures and abbreviations.

$27,565,000	NOT	$27,565,-000
CG&E	NOT	CG-&E

6.13 Do not divide the last word on a page. Avoid dividing the last word on more than two consecutive lines and the last word of a paragraph.

WORD HYPHENATION

The following rules are basic to hyphenation of words. When in doubt, refer to the dictionary.

6.14 Hyphenate a spelled-out compound number from 21 to 99.

twenty-one	forty-three
ninety-one	sixty-six

6.15 Hyphenate a compound adjective that immediately precedes a noun. Do not hyphenate if it follows a noun.

hard-to-get items	follow-up report
fire-resistant insulation	well-known author

6.16 Hyphenate words that are formed with the prefixes *all-*, *ex-*, *great-*, *half-*, and *self-*.

all-inclusive	ex-governor
great-grandmother	half-baked
self-control	

6.17 Hyphenate a word that might otherwise be misunderstood by the reader.

| re-create (to create again) | recreate (to refresh) |
| re-cover (to cover again) | recover (to regain) |

6.18 Hyphenate spelled-out fractions used as adjectives.

A one-half share was given to each new player.
In order for the bill to pass, a two-thirds vote is necessary.

6.19 Do not hyphenate a spelled-out fraction used as a noun.

One fourth of the students were missing because of illness.
He ate one fourth of the pie at one sitting.

6.20 Do not hyphenate titles and official positions.

| vice president | editor in chief |
| lieutenant governor | general manager |

6.21 As a rule do not hyphenate words formed with the prefixes *anti-, bi-, circum-, fore-, inter-, mis-, mono-, over-, super-, tri-, under-, uni-, up-,* and *where-.*

antitrust	circumnavigate
bicentennial	interstate
forewarn	monorail
mismatch	supervisor
oversimplify	underdeveloped
triangular	upright
unilateral	whereabouts

6.22 Hyphenate words formed with the prefixes *ante-, anti-, non-, post-, pre-, pro-, semi-,* and *un-* if the other element is a proper noun.

ante-Victorian	anti-Semitic
non-Indian	post-World War II
pre-Columbian	pro-British
semi-Americanized	trans-Siberian
un-Christian	

6.23 Do not hyphenate a combination of an adverb ending in *-ly* and an adjective that immediately precedes a noun.

| slowly rising water | quietly played song |
| eagerly awaited response | rapidly falling snow |

Self-Check Exercise

SECTION I

In the space beside each word, rewrite the word indicating with a hyphen the *first* acceptable division point. If the word cannot be divided, simply rewrite the entire word in the blank.

Example: manufacture ___manu-facture___   score _____score_____

1. complete _____

2. slapped _____

3. absolutely _____

4. tripping _____

5. falling _____

6. self-addressed _____

7. tentacle _____

8. stimulate _____

9. evaluation _____

10. through _____

SECTION II

By writing yes or no in the blanks, indicate whether the words below have been properly divided.

1. _____ in-to
2. _____ idealistical-ly
3. _____ manip-ulate
4. _____ Mrs. / Harriet Stowe
5. _____ NAA-CP

6. _____ e-vangelical
7. _____ manu-script
8. _____ wrap-ped
9. _____ state-hood
10. _____ applica-tion

SECTION III

In the space provided, rewrite any of the following words that are incorrectly presented.

Example: thirty two ___thirty-two___

1. grand-father _____

2. anti-British _____

3. trade-in-value _____

4. self control _____

5. superintendent _____

6. ex-president _____

7. up-standing _____

8. blue green water _____

9. two-thirds vote _____

10. pre-determine _____

Check your answers in the back of the book.

7 Spelling and Word Choice

IT IS IMPORTANT to be able to produce letters, memos, reports, and other forms of business communications that are free of spelling errors. While there are a number of basic spelling rules, most of them have exceptions. The best practice to follow to ensure correctly spelled words is to refer to a dictionary or a listing of words whenever you are in doubt.

PREFIXES

7.1 Knowing the meaning of prefixes may help you determine the meaning of words and their spelling. The most common prefixes, their meanings, and some examples follow.

ante- (before)
  antechamber
  antedate
anti- (against)
  antibiotic
  antitrust
bi- (two)
  bilateral
  bilingual
circum- (around)
  circumference
  circumstance
co- (together)
  co-educational
  cooperate
contra- (opposite; against)
  contraband
  contradiction
counter- (opposing)
  counteract
  counterclockwise
de- (removal; reversal)
  deactivate
  decontaminate

dis- (lack of)
  disability
  disagreement
ex- (removal; former; out)
  excavate
  exception
extra- (beyond)
  extracurricular
  extraordinary
fore- (before; front)
  foregoing
  foremost
hyper- (excessive)
  hyperactive
  hypertension
inter- (between)
  interoffice
  interstate
intra- (within)
  intramural
  intrastate
micro- (very small)
  microfilm
  microorganism

7

mid- (middle)
  midday
  midpoint
mis- (wrongness; opposite)
  misbehave
  misinform
mono- (one; single)
  monologue
  monopoly
multi- (many)
  multicolored
  multimedia
non- (not)
  noncommital
  nonconformist
out- (external; excel)
  outbreak
  outdistance
over- (excessive)
  overbearing
  overestimate
post- (after)
  postdate
  postgraduate
pre- (before)
  premature
  prepaid

pro- (favor; before)
  pro-American
  program
re- (again)
  reapportion
  rebuild
semi- (half of; partly)
  semicircle
  semiskilled
sub- (below)
  submarine
  substandard
super- (above)
  superhuman
  superstructure
trans- (across)
  transatlantic
  transcontinental
tri- (three)
  triangular
  tripod
un- (opposite of)
  unadvertised
  unannounced

SUFFIXES

7.2 Suffixes are word endings that form new words from base words. Knowing the meaning and spelling of suffixes will help you expand your vocabulary. Common suffixes, their meanings, and some examples follow.

-able (capable of being)
  debatable
  marketable
-age (connection with; place for)
  bondage
  leverage
-er, -or (one who; that which)
  bookkeeper
  creditor

-ful (abundance; having characteristics)
  deceitful
  masterful
-ian (resembling; skilled in)
  Bostonian
  mathematician
-less (lack of)
  blameless
  hopeless

-ly (resembling; in a specified manner)
   brotherly
   gradually
-ment (act of; state of)
   environment
   settlement

-ness (state; quality; condition)
   kindness
   quietness
-tion (action; process)
   absorption
   transaction

FORMING PLURALS

7.3 Most nouns take different forms to indicate singular or plural number. The singular form indicates only one person, place, or thing. The plural form indicates more than one person, place, or thing. The following rules relate to the formation of plurals. When in doubt about the formation of a plural, it is best to refer to a dictionary.

7.4 Most nouns form their plurals by adding *s* to the singular form. Noun plurals are *never* formed by adding *'s*.

Singular	Plural
accountant	accountants
desk	desks
table	tables

7.5 Nouns that end in *s, z, x, ch,* or *sh* form their plurals by adding *es* to the singular form.

Singular	Plural
loss	losses
tax	taxes
church	churches
brush	brushes

7.6 Nouns that end in *y* and are preceded by a consonant form their plurals by changing the *y* to *i* and adding *es*.

Singular	Plural
agency	agencies
lady	ladies
party	parties

Nouns that end in *y* and are preceded by a vowel form their plurals by adding *s*.

Singular	Plural
attorney	attorneys
valley	valleys

7.7 Most nouns that end in *f* or *fe* form their plurals by changing the *f* or *fe* to *v* and adding *es*.

Singular	Plural
half	halves
knife	knives
wife	wives

Some nouns that end in *f* form their plurals simply by adding *s*.

Singular	Plural
chief	chiefs
roof	roofs
sheriff	sheriffs

7.8 Most nouns that end in *o* form their plurals by adding *es* to the singular form.

Singular	Plural
echo	echoes
hero	heroes
tomato	tomatoes

Some nouns that end in *o* form their plurals by adding *s* to the singular form.

Singular	Plural
photo	photos
piano	pianos
radio	radios

7.9 Some nouns form their plurals by changing a letter or letters within the singular form or by adding a special ending.

Singular	Plural
foot	feet
man	men
child	children
ox	oxen

7.10 Some words derived from other languages use special endings to form their plurals.

Singular	Plural
alumnus	alumni
datum	data
nucleus	nuclei

7.11 Some nouns retain the same form for both singular and plural.

Singular	Plural
fish	fish
quail	quail
sheep	sheep

Some nouns have only one form and may be used for both singular and plural number.

goods	scissors
headquarters	series
news	thanks

7.12 Compound words written as single words form their plurals in the regular way.

Singular	Plural
bookkeeper	bookkeepers
handful	handfuls
stockbroker	stockbrokers

Hyphenated compound nouns generally form their plurals by changing the main word in the compound to the plural form.

Singular	Plural
attorney-at-law	attorneys-at-law
mother-in-law	mothers-in-law

WORD CHOICE

7.13 The proper selection of words is important to successful business communication. Special care must be taken with words that look alike or that sound alike. Refer to a dictionary if more specific meanings are needed.

accede (agree to)
exceed (surpass)

accent (emphasize; give prominence to)
ascend (climb)
ascent (advancement)
assent (agree with)

accept (receive; agree)
except (exclude)

adapt (adjust; revise)
adept (highly skilled)
adopt (take by choice)

addition (increase; attachment)
edition (publication)

adverse (unfavorable)
averse (opposed)

advice (n., recommendation; guidance)
advise (v., give information; suggest)

affect (v., influence)
effect (n., result)
effect (v., bring about; cause)

aid (help; comfort)
aide (assistant)

aisle (passageway)
isle (island)

allowed (permitted)
aloud (audibly)

all ready (completely prepared)
already (by now)

all together (including all)
altogether (completely)

allude (refer to)
elude (escape; avoid)

altar (worship table)
alter (change)

any one (*any* person)
anyone (any *one* person or thing in a group)

are (form of verb *be*)
hour (60 minutes)
our (possessive form of *we*)

assure (convince)
ensure (guarantee)
insure (protect against loss)

attendance (people present)
attendants (assistants)

bases (reasons; foundations)
basis (a reason; a foundation)

biannual (twice a year)
biennial (every two years)

born (given birth)
borne (carried)

brake (n., stopping device)
break (v., separate into parts)

breadth (width)
breath (the air inhaled and exhaled)
breathe (inhale and exhale)

buy (purchase)
by (next to; close to)

canvas (n., heavy cloth)
canvass (v., solicit)

capital (most important; city that is official seat of government)
capitol (a building for a legislature)

carton (cardboard box)
cartoon (a drawing)

ceiling (top; limit)
sealing (closing securely)

cent (penny)
scent (odor)
sent (dispatched)

cite (quote)
sight (vision)
site (location)

coarse (rough)
course (plan; pattern)

collision (crash)
collusion (fraudulent secret agreement)

command (control)
commend (compliment)

complement (add to)
compliment (praise)

conscience (one's moral sense)
conscious (aware of)

consul   (foreign representative)
council   (governing body)
counsel   (n., advice)
counsel   (v., to give advice)

costume   (dress)
custom   (tradition)

datum   (information, singular)
data   (information, plural)

decease   (die)
disease   (sickness)

decent   (having moral qualities)
descend   (move downward)
descent   (a downward step)
dissent   (disagreement)

deprecate   (disapprove of)
depreciate   (lessen)

desert   (n., wilderness)
desert   (v., abandon)
dessert   (n., food)

device   (n., equipment)
devise   (v., to plan)

die   (cease living)
dye   (color)

disapprove   (have an unfavor-
                 able opinion)
disprove   (show to be false)

disburse   (pay out)
disperse   (scatter)

elicit   (ask for)
illicit (illegal)

eligible   (qualified)
illegible   (unreadable)

emerge   (come forth)
immerge   (plunge into)

emigrate   (leave a country)
immigrate   (come into a country)

eminent   (prominent)
imminent   (about to happen)

envelop   (surround)
envelope   (container for a letter)

expand   (increase)
expend   (pay out)

farther   (at a greater distance)
further   (more; in addition)

fiscal   (financial)
physical   (of material things)

forego   (go before)
forgo   (relinquish; give up)

foreword   (preface)
forward   (at the front)

formally   (ceremoniously)
formerly   (at an earlier time)

forth   (first; ahead)
fourth   (after third)

grate   (n., a grill)
grate   (v., shred)
great   (large; distinguished)

guarantee   (make sure)
guaranty   (contract; certificate)

guessed   (estimated; supposed)
guest   (welcome visitor)

hear   (listen)
here   (at this place)

higher   (taller; greater)
hire   (employ)

hole   (an opening)
whole   (entire; complete)

incite   (encourage; arouse)
insight   (an understanding of)

instance   (example; event)
instants   (moments)

interstate   (between states)
intrastate   (within one state)

its   (possessive form of *it*)
it's   (it is)

knew   (was aware of)
new   (not old)

later   (more recent)
latter   (second of two)

lay   (place; sit)
lie   (be situated)

lead   (n., metal; first place)
lead   (v., guide; precede)
led   (v., taken; escorted)

lean   (bend; rely on)
lien   (legal claim)

leased   (rented)
least   (smallest)

lessen   (make smaller)
lesson   (instruction)

lesser   (smaller)
lessor   (landlord)

liable   (responsible)
libel   (written slander)

loan   (something lent)
lone   (only one)

loose   (not tight)
lose   (misplace)

marital   (pertaining to marriage)
marshal   (legal officer)
martial   (military)

may be   (can be)
maybe   (perhaps)

miner   (n., worker in a mine)
minor   (adj., smaller amount)
minor   (n., under legal age)

moral   (legal; ethical)
morale   (spirit)

ordinance   (law)
ordnance   (military supplies)

passed   (overtook)
past   (over; gone by)

patience   (tolerance)
patients   (those under medical care)

persecuted   (mistreated)
prosecuted   (sued in court)

personal   (private)
personnel   (workers; staff)

perspective   (point of view)
prospective   (hoped for)

plain   (lacking ornament)
plane   (level)

practicable   (possible)
practical   (useful)

precede   (go before)
proceed   (continue)

prescribe   (give directions)
proscribe   (forbid; condemn)

presence   (attendance)
presents   (gifts)

principal   (major; main)
principle   (rule)

profit   (benefit; gain)
prophet   (one who predicts)

reality   (truth)
realty   (real estate)

seize   (take)
siege   (battle)

set   (place; put)
sit   (take a seat)

stationary   (in the same place)
stationery   (writing paper)

than   (compared to)
then   (at that time)

their   (possessive form of *they*)
there   (in that place)
they're   (they are)

threw	(tossed)
through	(by way of)
to	(in the direction of)
too	(in addition to; also)
two	(one and one)
waist	(middle of the body)
waste	(n., unusable material)
waste	(v., squander)
waive	(give up)
wave	(signal)
ware	(material goods)
wear	(have on)
where	(at what place)
weak	(without strength)
week	(seven days)
weather	(climate)
whether	(if)
who's	(who is)
whose	(possessive form of *who*)
your	(possessive form of *you*)
you're	(you are)

COMMONLY MISSPELLED WORDS

7.14   The following list contains words that are often misspelled. All the words in the list are presented showing acceptable word division points.

A

ab-bre-vi-ate	ade-quate	amount
abey-ance	ad-ja-cent	analy-sis
abili-ties	ad-journed	ana-lyze
ab-sence	ad-just-able	an-nexa-tion
ab-stract	ad-just-ment	an-nounce-ment
ac-cel-er-ate	ad-min-is-ter	an-nual
ac-cept-able	ad-min-is-tra-tion	anony-mous
ac-ces-si-ble	ad-vance-ment	an-swer
ac-ces-sory	ad-ver-tise-ment	an-tici-pate
ac-ci-dent	ad-vice	anti-trust
ac-com-mo-date	ad-vis-able	anx-ious
ac-com-pany	ad-vise	apolo-gize
ac-count-ant	ad-vi-sory	ap-pa-ra-tus
ac-crual	ad-vo-cate	ap-parel
ac-cu-mu-late	af-fi-da-vit	ap-par-ent
ac-cu-racy	af-fili-ation	ap-pear-ance
ac-cu-rate	af-firma-tive	ap-pen-dix
ac-cus-tom	af-ford	ap-pli-ance
achieve-ment	agency	ap-pli-ca-ble
ac-knowl-edge	align-ment	ap-pli-cant
ac-knowl-edg-ment	al-lot-ment	ap-pli-ca-tion
ac-quain-tance	al-low-ance	ap-point-ment
ac-qui-si-tion	al-ready	ap-praisal
ac-tu-arial	al-tera-tion	ap-praise
adapt-able	al-ter-na-tive	ap-pre-ci-ate
ad-di-tion	al-though	ap-pren-tice
ad-dress	al-to-gether	ap-proach
ad-dressed	amend-ment	ap-pro-pri-ate
	am-or-ti-za-tion	ap-proval

ap-prove
ap-proxi-mate
ap-ti-tude
ar-bi-tra-tion
ar-gu-ment
ar-range-ment
ar-rears
ar-ti-cle
ar-ti-fi-cial
as-cer-tain
as-sem-bly
as-sess-ment
as-ses-sor
asset
as-sign-ment
as-sis-tant
as-so-ci-ate
as-so-cia-tion
as-sort-ment
as-sume
at-tached
at-tach-ment
at-tain-able
at-tempt
at-ten-dance
at-ten-tion
at-ti-tude
at-tor-ney
au-di-ence
au-di-tor
au-di-to-rium
au-then-tic
au-thori-za-tion
au-thor-ize
auto-matic
auto-mo-bile
aux-il-iary
avail-able
aware-ness

B
bac-ca-lau-re-ate
bal-ance
bank-rupt
bank-ruptcy
ban-quet
bar-gain
ba-rome-ter
basi-cally
bear-ing
beau-ti-ful
be-gin-ning
be-hav-ior
be-lief
be-lieve

bel-lig-er-ent
be-long-ings
bene-fac-tor
bene-fi-cial
bene-fi-ci-ary
bene-fit
bene-fited
be-nevo-lent
be-wil-dered
bib-li-og-ra-phy
bi-en-nium
bill-board
bill-ing
bil-lion
bi-monthly
bi-nary
bi-og-ra-phy
bio-log-ical
blem-ish
blend-ing
blue-print
bod-ily
bol-ster
bom-bard
bona fide
bonus
book-keeper
book-let
booth
bor-row
bot-tle-neck
boule-vard
bound-ary
boun-ti-ful
boy-cott
breach
break-age
brief
bril-liant
broad-cast
broaden
bro-chure
bro-ker
bro-ker-age
brought
budget
budg-et-ary
bul-le-tin
bun-dle
bur-den
bu-reau
bu-reauc-racy
bu-reau-crat
bur-glary
busi-ness

busi-ness-man
busi-ness-woman
by-laws

C
cabi-net
cal-cu-late
cal-en-dar
cali-ber
cam-paign
can-cel
can-celed
can-cel-la-tion
can-did
can-di-date
ca-pa-ble
ca-pac-ity
capi-tal
capi-tal-ize
capi-tol
card-board
ca-reer
care-ful
care-less
car-load
car-rier
car-ton
car-tridge
cash-ier
cas-ual
cata-logue
cata-lyst
ca-tas-tro-phe
cate-gory
cau-tion
cease
ceil-ing
cele-brate
ce-leb-rity
cen-sor
cen-ti-grade
cen-ti-me-ter
cen-tral
cere-mony
cer-tain
cer-tifi-cate
cer-tify
chal-lenge
chaos
chap-ter
char-ac-ter
charge-able
chari-ta-ble
char-ity
chas-sis

chem-ical
chief
chrono-log-ical
cir-cuit
cir-cu-lar
cir-cu-late
ci-ta-tion
citi-zen
claim-ant
clar-ify
clas-sify
cler-ical
cli-ent
cli-en-tele
cog-ni-zant
co-in-cide
co-in-sur-ance
col-labo-rate
col-lapse
col-lat-eral
col-league
col-lec-tion
col-lec-tive
col-li-sion
col-lu-sion
col-umn
co-lum-nar
com-bi-na-tion
com-fort-able
com-memo-rate
com-mend
com-ment
com-mer-cial
com-mis-sion
com-mit
com-mit-tee
com-mod-ity
com-mu-ni-cate
com-mu-nism
com-mu-nity
com-mute
com-pany
com-pa-ra-ble
com-para-tive
com-part-ment
com-pat-ible
com-pen-sate
com-pe-tent
com-pe-ti-tion
com-peti-tive
com-peti-tor
com-pile
com-plain
com-plete
com-pli-cate

com-pli-ment
com-pli-men-tary
com-ply
com-po-nent
com-pound
com-pre-hen-sive
com-prise
com-pro-mise
comp-trol-ler
com-pul-sory
com-pu-ta-tion
com-pute
com-puter
con-ceal
con-cede
con-ceived
con-cen-trate
con-cept
con-ces-sion
con-clude
con-cur
con-di-tion
con-duct
con-duit
con-fer-ence
con-fide
con-fi-dent
con-fi-den-tial
con-fir-ma-tion
con-flict
con-fuse
con-gratu-late
con-gress
con-gres-sional
con-nect
con-sci-en-tious
con-scious
con-secu-tive
con-sen-sus
con-se-quence
con-ser-va-tive
con-serve
con-sider
con-sign
con-signee
con-sign-ment
con-sis-tent
con-soli-date
con-sor-tium
con-spicu-ous
con-stitu-ent
con-sti-tute
con-sult
con-sult-ant
con-sume

con-sumer
con-tem-plate
con-tem-po-rary
con-text
con-ti-nen-tal
con-tin-gency
con-tinue
con-ti-nu-ity
con-tract
con-trac-tor
con-trac-tual
con-tra-dict
con-trast
con-trib-ute
con-tro-ver-sial
con-ven-ience
con-ven-ient
con-ven-tion
con-ver-sion
con-vert-ible
con-vey
con-vey-ance
con-vic-tion
co-op-er-ate
co-or-di-nate
co-owner
cor-dial
cor-po-ra-tion
cor-rec-tion
cor-re-late
cor-re-spond
cor-re-spon-dence
cor-re-spon-dents
cor-robo-rate
cor-ro-sion
coun-cil
coun-sel
coun-ter-feit
cou-pon
cour-te-ous
cour-tesy
cov-er-age
co-worker
cre-den-tials
credi-bil-ity
credi-tor
crimi-nal
cri-te-ria
cri-te-rion
criti-cism
criti-cize
cru-cial
crys-tal-lize
cul-mi-nate
cul-ti-vate

cu-mu-la-tive
cur-rency
cur-ricu-lum
cur-tail
cus-tody
cus-tom-ary
cycle

D
dan-ger-ous
de-bat-able
de-ben-ture
debit
de-bris
debtor
de-ce-dent
de-ceive
deci-mal
de-ci-sion
de-ci-sive
dec-la-ra-tion
de-cline
deco-ra-tion
dedi-cate
de-duct
de-duct-ible
de-duc-tion
de-fault
de-fec-tive
de-fen-dant
defer
de-fer-ral
de-fi-ciency
defi-cit
defi-nite
defi-ni-tion
dele-gate
dele-ga-tion
de-lib-er-ate
de-li-cious
de-light-ful
de-lin-quent
de-liv-ery
de-moc-racy
de-mol-ish
dem-on-strate
dem-on-stra-tion
de-nomi-na-tion
de-note
de-part-ment
de-part-men-tal
de-par-ture
de-pend-able
de-pend-ent
de-pict

de-plete
de-posi-tor
de-pre-ci-ate
de-pres-sion
de-scribe
de-scrip-tion
de-sir-able
de-spite
des-ti-na-tion
des-ti-tute
de-struc-tion
de-tach
de-te-rio-rate
de-ter-mine
de-valu-ation
de-velop
de-vel-op-ment
de-vi-ate
di-ag-nose
di-ag-no-sis
dla-gram
di-ame-ter
dic-ta-tion
dic-tion-ary
dif-fer-ence
dif-fer-ent
dif-fi-cult
dif-fi-culty
di-lem-ma
dili-gent
di-men-sion
di-min-ish
di-rec-tory
dis-ad-van-tage
disa-gree
dis-ap-pear
dis-ap-point
dis-burse-ment
dis-clo-sure
dis-con-tinue
dis-cour-age
dis-cov-ery
dis-crep-ancy
dis-crimi-nate
dis-cus-sion
dis-honest
dis-or-gan-ized
dis-pos-able
dis-po-si-tion
dis-pute
dis-sat-is-fac-tion
dis-semi-nate
dis-so-lu-tion
dis-tinct
dis-tin-guish

dis-trib-ute
dis-tri-bu-tion
dis-tribu-tor
dis-trict
di-ver-sify
divi-dend
di-vi-sion
docu-ment
do-mes-tic
do-na-tion
doubt-ful
dra-matic
drudg-ery
dual
du-pli-cate
du-ra-tion
dy-namic

E
ear-lier
ease-ment
eas-ily
eco-nomic
eco-no-mist
econo-mize
econ-omy
edi-tion
edi-to-rial
edu-cate
ef-fect
ef-fec-tive
ef-fi-cient
ef-fort
elabo-rate
elec-tion
elec-tor-ate
elec-tric
elec-tronic
ele-men-tary
ele-va-tion
eli-gi-ble
elimi-nate
em-bar-rass
em-bez-zle
emer-gency
emo-tional
em-pha-size
em-ployee
em-ploy-ment
en-clo-sure
en-coun-ter
en-cour-age
en-cy-clo-pe-dia
en-dan-ger
en-deavor

en-dorse
en-dorse-ment
en-dow-ment
en-gage-ment
en-gi-neer
en-joy-able
en-ter-prise
en-ter-tain-ment
en-thu-si-asm
en-tice-ment
en-ti-tle
en-tre-pre-neur
entry
en-ve-lope
en-vi-able
en-vi-ron-ment
equip-ment
equipped
eq-ui-ta-ble
eq-uity
equiva-lent
er-ro-ne-ous
es-crow
es-pe-cially
es-sen-tial
es-tab-lish
es-ti-mate
evalu-ate
evapo-rate
eva-sive
even-tual
evi-dence
evo-lu-tion
ex-ag-ger-ate
ex-ami-na-tion
ex-cel-lent
ex-cep-tion
ex-cerpt
ex-ces-sive
ex-clude
ex-clu-sive
exe-cute
ex-ecu-tive
ex-ecu-tor
ex-em-plify
ex-empt
ex-emp-tion
ex-er-cise
exert
ex-haust
ex-hibit
ex-hi-bi-tion
ex-or-bi-tant
ex-pand
ex-pe-dite

ex-pend-able
ex-pen-di-ture
ex-pe-ri-ence
ex-peri-ment
ex-plain
ex-pla-na-tion
ex-plicit
ex-plore
ex-press
ex-tent
ex-te-rior
ex-ter-nal
ex-tinct
ex-tin-guish
ex-tor-tion
ex-tract
ex-traor-di-nary
ex-trava-gant

F

fab-ri-cate
fa-cili-tate
fa-cili-ties
fac-sim-ile
fal-sify
fa-mil-iar
fa-mil-iar-ize
fas-ci-nated
fa-vor-able
fea-si-bil-ity
fea-si-ble
feed-back
fel-low-ship
femi-nine
fic-tional
fic-ti-tious
fi-del-ity
fi-du-ci-ary
fi-nal-ize
fi-nan-cial
fin-an-cier
fis-cal
flex-ible
fluc-tu-ate
flu-ent
fluo-res-cent
focus
for-bear-ance
for-bid-den
for-ci-bly
fore-cast
fore-clo-sure
forego
for-eign
fore-see-able

fore-sight
fore-stall
for-feit
for-gery
for-ma-tion
for-mi-da-ble
for-mula
for-tu-nate
for-ward
foun-da-tion
frag-ile
frag-ment
fran-chise
fraud
fraudu-lent
freight
fre-quency
fre-quent
fringe
frus-tra-tion
ful-fill
func-tion
fun-da-men-tal
fur-nish

G

gen-eral
gen-er-ate
gen-er-ous
genu-ine
geo-graphic
gi-gan-tic
gov-ern
gov-ern-ment
gov-er-nor
gra-cious
gra-di-ent
grad-ual
gram-mar
grate-ful
grati-fied
griev-ance
grieve
gross
guar-an-tee
guar-anty
guard-ian
gu-ber-na-to-rial
gui-dance

H

habi-tat
ha-bit-ual
handi-capped
hand-ker-chief

hap-haz-ard
hap-pi-ness
har-ass
hast-ily
haz-ard
haz-ard-ous
head-quar-ters
height
help-ful
he-redi-tary
here-to-fore
heri-tage
hesi-tate
het-ero-ge-ne-ous
his-toric
ho-mo-ge-ne-ous
hon-or-able
hope-ful
hori-zon-tal
hos-pi-tal-ity
hos-tile
house-hold
hu-man-ity
hu-mor-ous
hun-dred-weight
hy-pothe-sis

I

iden-ti-cal
iden-ti-fi-ca-tion
iden-tify
ig-ni-tion
il-le-gal
il-leg-ible
il-le-giti-mate
il-lit-er-ate
il-lu-mi-nate
il-lu-sion
il-lus-trate
il-lus-tra-tion
im-agi-na-tion
imi-ta-tion
im-ma-te-rial
im-me-di-ate
im-mense
im-mi-grant
im-par-tial
im-passe
im-pa-tient
im-pend-ing
im-pera-tive
im-per-fect
im-ple-ment
im-por-tance
im-prac-ti-cal

im-prob-ably
im-proper
im-prove-ment
im-pulse
ina-bil-ity
in-ac-cu-rate
in-ac-tive
in-ade-quate
in-ad-vis-able
in-ap-pro-pri-ate
in-ar-ticu-late
in-as-much
in-au-gu-rate
in-cen-tive
in-cep-tion
in-ci-dent
in-clem-ent
in-cli-na-tion
in-com-pa-ra-ble
in-com-pe-tent
in-con-clu-sive
in-con-sis-tent
in-con-ven-ience
in-cor-po-rate
in-cre-ment
in-cum-bent
incur
in-debt-ed-ness
in-defi-nite
in-de-pend-ence
in-di-cate
in-dis-pen-sa-ble
in-di-vid-ual
in-duce-ment
in-dulge
in-ef-fi-cient
in-equi-ties
in-ex-pen-sive
in-fal-li-ble
in-fi-nite
in-fla-tion
in-flu-ence
in-fre-quent
in-fringe-ment
in-gre-di-ent
ini-tial
ini-ti-ate
ini-tia-tive
in-quiry
in-sig-nifi-cant
in-spec-tion
in-stal-la-tion
in-stall-ment
in-sti-tu-tion
in-stru-ment

in-suf-fi-cient
in-sur-mount-able
in-tan-gi-ble
in-te-grate
in-tel-li-gent
in-ten-tional
in-ter-de-pen-dent
in-ter-fer-ence
in-ter-me-di-ate
in-ter-na-tional
in-ter-pret
in-ter-rupt
in-ter-state
in-tes-tate
in-tra-state
in-tro-duce
in-valid
in-ves-ti-gate
in-vest-ment
in-ves-tor
in-vi-ta-tion
in-voice
ir-re-spon-si-ble
item-ize
item-ized
itin-er-ary

J

jeop-ard-ize
job-ber
jour-nal
judg-ment
ju-di-cial
ju-di-ci-ary
jur-is-dic-tion
jus-tice
jus-ti-fi-ca-tion

K

key-board
key-punch
kilo-watt
knowl-edge
knowl-edge-able

L

label
labo-ra-tory
lan-guage
lapse
lati-tude
law-suit
leaf-let
lease
ledger

legal
le-gal-ity
leg-ible
leg-is-late
leg-is-la-tion
le-giti-mate
lei-sure
le-ni-ent
let-ter-head
lia-bil-ity
lia-ble
li-ai-son
libel
lib-eral
li-brary
li-cense
li-cen-see
lien
like-li-hood
limi-ta-tion
li-qui-date
lit-er-ally
liti-ga-tion
live-li-hood
lo-cal-ity
lo-ca-tion
log-ical
lon-gi-tude
lu-cra-tive

M
ma-chin-ery
mag-ni-tude
mail-able
main-tain
main-te-nance
ma-jor-ity
man-age-able
man-age-ment
mana-ger-ial
man-da-tory
mani-fest
ma-nipu-late
manu-fac-ture
mar-ginal
mar-ket-able
ma-te-rial
ma-tur-ity
maxi-mum
meas-ure-ment
me-chan-ical
me-dia-tor
memo-ran-dum
mer-can-tile
mer-chan-dise

mer-chant
merger
me-tro-poli-tan
mi-cro-film
mil-li-me-ter
mime-ograph
mini-ature
mini-mal
mi-nor-ity
mis-cel-la-ne-ous
mis-in-ter-pret
mis-rep-re-sent
mis-un-der-stand-ing
miti-ga-tion
mod-er-ate
mod-ern-ize
mod-est
mo-men-tary
moni-tor
moral
mo-rale
mora-to-rium
mor-tal-ity
mort-gage
mort-ga-gee
mort-ga-gor
mo-ti-vate
mu-nici-pal
mu-nici-pal-ity
mu-tual

N
naive
nec-es-sary
ne-ces-si-tate
ne-ces-sity
nega-tive
ne-glect
neg-li-gent
ne-go-tia-ble
neigh-bor-hood
nev-er-the-less
night-mare
no-men-cla-ture
nomi-nal
nomi-na-tion
non-profit
no-tary
no-tice-able
not-with-stand-ing
nui-sance
nu-mer-ical

O
oath

ob-jec-tion
ob-jec-tive
ob-li-gate
ob-li-ga-tion
ob-ser-va-tion
ob-so-lete
ob-sta-cle
ob-struc-tion
oc-ca-sion
oc-ca-sion-ally
oc-cu-pant
oc-cu-pa-tion
oc-cur-rence
omis-sion
op-er-ate
op-era-tion
op-por-tu-nity
op-ti-mis-tic
or-di-nance
or-gani-za-tion
ori-en-ta-tion
origi-nal
os-ten-ta-tious
over-due
over-whelm-ing

P
pam-phlet
para-graph
par-al-lel
para-phrase
par-lia-men-tary
par-tici-pant
par-tici-pate
par-ticu-lar
part-ner-ship
pat-ent
pa-tience
pat-tern
pay-able
pe-des-trian
per-ceive
per-cent-age
per-cep-tive
per-fo-rate
per-form-ance
pe-ri-od-ical
per-ish-able
per-ma-nent
per-mis-sion
per-se-ver-ance
per-sonal
per-son-al-ity
per-son-nel
per-sua-sion

per-sua-sive
per-ti-nent
pe-ti-tion
pe-tro-leum
phe-nome-nal
phi-loso-phy
pho-to-copy
pho-tog-ra-phy
phys-ical
pil-fer-age
plain-tiff
plead-ings
pleas-ure
pneu-matic
poli-cy-hol-der
poli-ti-cian
popu-la-tion
port-folio
pos-sess
pos-ses-sion
pos-si-ble
post-dated
po-ten-tial
pov-erty
prac-ti-cal
prac-tice
pre-cau-tion
prece-dent
pre-ci-sion
pre-de-ter-mined
pref-er-able
preju-dice
pre-limi-nary
pre-ma-ture
pre-mium
prepa-ra-tion
pre-req-ui-site
pre-roga-tive
pre-scribe
pres-en-ta-tion
pre-vi-ous
pri-mary
prin-ci-pal
prin-ci-ple
pri-or-ity
privi-lege
prob-able
pro-ce-dure
pro-ceed
pro-cess
pro-cured
pro-duce
pro-duc-tion
pro-fes-sion
pro-fi-cient

profit
prof-it-able
pro-hibit
proj-ect
promi-nent
prom-ise
prom-is-sory
pro-mo-tion
prompt
pro-nounce
propa-ganda
prop-erty
pro-po-nent
pro-por-tion
pro-posal
pro-prie-tor
pro-prie-tor-ship
pro rata
prose-cu-tion
pros-pect
pro-tec-tion
pro-vide
pro-vi-sion
proxy
pub-li-ca-tion
punc-tual
pur-su-ant

Q
quad-ru-pli-cate
quali-fi-ca-tion
qual-ity
quan-tity
quar-terly
ques-tion-naire
quota
quo-ta-tion

R
rad-ical
rami-fi-ca-tion
rati-fi-ca-tion
re-ac-tion
read-ily
re-al-ity
re-al-ize
re-alty
rea-son-able
re-as-sign
re-ca-pitu-la-tion
re-ceipt
re-ceiv-able
re-ceive
re-ceiv-er-ship

re-cep-tion-ist
re-cep-tive
re-ces-sion
re-cipi-ent
re-cip-ro-cal
re-cip-ro-cate
rec-og-ni-tion
rec-om-mend
rec-om-men-da-tion
rec-on-cile
re-con-di-tion
re-cov-ery
re-cur-rence
re-deem-able
re-de-sign
re-duc-tion
re-elec-tion
refe-ree
ref-er-ence
re-fer-ral
re-fi-nance
re-fin-ery
re-gard-less
reg-is-ter
reg-is-try
regu-la-tion
re-ha-bili-ta-tion
re-im-burse
re-in-state
re-it-er-ate
re-la-tion
re-la-tion-ship
rele-vant
re-li-able
re-lief
re-lin-quish
re-lo-ca-tion
re-luc-tant
re-mark-able
re-me-dial
rem-edy
re-mit-tance
rem-nant
re-mov-able
re-mu-nera-tion
re-ne-go-ti-ate
reno-vate
repe-ti-tion
re-place-ment
rep-lica
re-pos-sess
rep-re-sent
rep-re-sen-ta-tive
re-pro-duce
repu-ta-ble

repu-ta-tion
req-ui-si-tion
re-scind
res-er-va-tion
resi-dence
resi-den-tial
res-ig-na-tion
re-sis-tant
reso-lu-tion
re-spect-able
re-spon-si-bil-ity
res-tau-rant
res-to-ra-tion
re-strict
re-sul-tant
re-trieval
ret-ro-ac-tive
re-turn-able
re-un-ion
reve-nue
re-vert
re-vise
re-voke
right-ful
ro-ta-tion
rou-tine

S
sac-ri-fice
sal-able
sal-ary
salu-ta-tion
sat-is-fac-tion
sat-is-fac-tory
sat-isfy
satu-rate
scar-city
sched-ule
sci-en-tific
sea-son-able
sec-on-dary
sec-re-tar-ial
sec-re-tary
sec-tional
se-cu-rity
se-lec-tion
self-addressed
self-employed
semi-annual
semi-monthly
sen-si-tive
sepa-rate
ser-vice-able
sev-er-ance
short-age

sig-na-ture
sig-nifi-cance
sig-nifi-cant
simi-lar
simi-lar-ity
sim-pli-fied
sim-plify
si-mul-ta-ne-ous
sin-cere
sin-cerely
sin-gu-lar
situ-ation
skill-ful
so-cial
so-cially
so-ci-ety
so-licit
so-lici-tor
soli-tary
so-lu-tion
sol-vent
so-phis-ti-cated
spe-cial-ist
spe-cial-ize
spe-cific
speci-fi-ca-tion
spec-tacu-lar
spec-trum
specu-la-tion
spon-sor
spon-ta-ne-ous
sta-bil-ity
stan-dard-ize
sta-tion-ary
sta-tion-ery
sta-tis-ti-cal
stat-utes
ste-nog-ra-pher
stimu-late
stipu-la-tion
straighten
stra-te-gic
sub-com-mit-tee
sub-con-trac-tor
sub-poena
sub-ro-ga-tion
sub-scrip-tion
sub-se-quent
sub-sidi-ary
sub-si-dize
sub-stan-tially
sub-sti-tute
sub-ur-ban
suc-cess
suf-fi-cient

suita-bil-ity
sum-ma-rize
su-per-in-ten-dent
su-per-sede
su-per-vise
sup-ple-ment
sur-tax
sym-bolic
sym-pathy
sys-tem

T
tabu-late
tan-gi-ble
tar-iff
tax-able
taxa-tion
tech-ni-cal
tech-ni-cal-ity
tech-ni-cian
tech-nique
tech-nol-ogy
tele-phone
tem-pera-ment
tem-pera-ture
tem-po-rary
ten-dency
ten-ta-tive
ter-mi-nate
ter-mi-nol-ogy
tes-ti-mony
thor-ough
thor-oughly
though
thought
threat-ened
through
tol-er-ant
tol-er-ate
to-taled
tour-na-ment
trac-tion
tra-di-tion
trag-edy
trans-ac-tion
tran-scribe
trans-fer
trans-fu-sion
tran-si-tion
trans-por-ta-tion
treas-urer
trip-li-cate
trus-tee
type-writer
typo-graph-ical

U
ul-ti-mate
ul-ti-ma-tum
un-ac-cus-tomed
unani-mous
un-at-trac-tive
un-be-liev-able
un-con-trol-la-ble
un-der-stand-able
un-der-writer
un-en-force-able
un-fa-mil-iar
un-fore-see-able
un-for-tu-nate
uni-form
uni-for-mity
unique
uni-ver-sal
un-man-age-able
un-prece-dented
un-pre-dict-able
un-sur-passed
ur-gent
util-ity
utili-za-tion

V
va-cant
va-ca-tion
vacuum
vali-da-tion
va-lid-ity
valu-ation
value
vari-able
vari-ation
ve-hi-cle
ven-ture
ver-bal
ver-ba-tim
veri-fi-ca-tion
ver-sa-tile
ver-sion
ver-ti-cal
vi-cin-ity
vig-or-ous
vio-late
visi-bil-ity
visu-al-ize
vo-cabu-lary
vol-un-teer
voucher

W
waive
ware-house
war-rant
war-ranty
where-fore
whole-sale
whole-some
with-draw
with-hold-ing
wit-ness
won-der-ful

X
x-ray

Y
yard-age
yes-ter-day
yield

Z
zero
zone

Self-Check Exercise

SECTION I

Complete the spelling of the following words by supplying the correct prefix or suffix. The meaning is shown in parentheses.

1. _____ trust (against)

2. _____ partisan (two)

3. _____ state (within)

4. _____ appropriate (wrongly)

5. _____ determine (before)

6. _____ port (across)

7. sleep_____ (lack of)

8. fashion_____ (capa-
   ble of being)

9. measure_____ (act of)

10. joy_____ (abundance)

SECTION II

Of the two meanings given for each word below, select the correct meaning by circling it.

1. accept   receive
   exclude

2. capital   seat of government
   a building

3. site   vision
   location

4. fiscal   financial
   of material things

5. formerly   at an earlier time
   ceremoniously

6. grate   a grill
   large

7. personnel   private
   workers

8. stationary   writing paper
   in the same place

9. moral   spirit
   legal

10. whether   climate
    if

SECTION III

Circle the correctly spelled word in the pairs of words below.

1. achievment
   achievement

2. alotment
   allotment

3. arrears
   arears

4. benefitted
   benefited

5. breakage
   brakage

6. budgetery
   budgetary

7. canselation
   cancellation
8. congradulate
   congratulate
9. creditor
   crediter
10. deductible
    deductable
11. depreciate
    deprecciate
12. endorsment
    endorsement
13. exaggerate
    exagerate
14. grievance
    grieveance
15. hazard
    hazzard
16. incoprate
    incorporate
17. judgment
    jugement
18. leger
    ledger

19. likelihood
    liklihood
20. mantenance
    maintenance
21. preferrable
    preferable
22. recommendation
    reccomendation
23. remitance
    remittance
24. sincerely
    sincerly
25. taxable
    taxeable
26. tenative
    tentative
27. unfamiliar
    unfamilar
28. unique
    uniquce
29. waranty
    warranty
30. wherefore
    wherfore

SECTION IV

Write the correct plural form in the blank.

1. swimmer   _____
2. switch   _____
3. rally   _____
4. journey   _____
5. shelf   _____

6. potato   _____
7. ox   _____
8. woman   _____
9. moose   _____
10. father-in-law _____

Check your answers in the back of the book.

8 Typing Techniques

ONE OF THE major tasks of office personnel is the preparation of various items—letters, memos, reports, agendas, forms, tables, etc. In order to perform well in this important area, attention must be given to organizing work and supplies, proofreading, correcting, making copies, using special techniques to speed routine tasks, and following acceptable form for the completion of the items.

ORGANIZATION OF MATERIALS

8.1 To be used effectively, materials must be organized so they are easily accessible. Arrange supplies so that they can be secured quickly and easily. Always keep enough supplies on hand so that work is not continually interrupted to obtain additional materials.

Divide the stationery used into separate sections—letterheads, carbon paper, copy paper, and plain paper. Store carbon paper in such a way that it will not wrinkle.

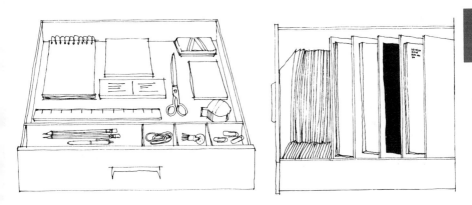

Figure 8-1   Organize your work area

Letterheads

8.2 Letterheads are generally printed on high-quality paper with the name and address of the company appearing at the top of each sheet. Letterheads may also include a telephone number, slogan, or logo.

They come in a variety of qualities and sizes. The most common sizes
are:

5½ × 8½ inches   Baronial or half-sized
7¼ × 10½ inches   Executive or monarch
8 × 10½ inches   Government
8½ × 11 inches   Business or standard

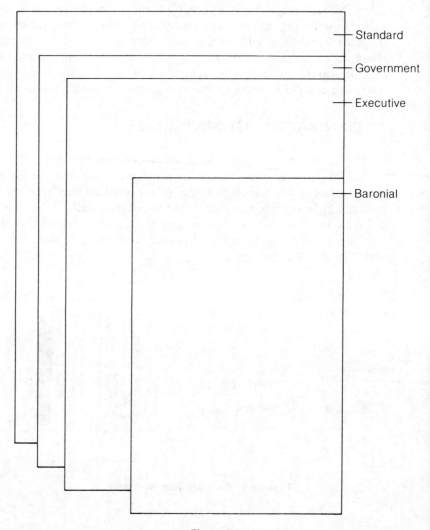

Figure 8-2

Baronial or half-sized letterheads are sometimes used in business for
very short messages. The *executive or monarch* size is most often used
by business executives or professional people for their business or

private correspondence. *Government* letterheads are used by government agencies and by the armed forces. The government is presently in the process of changing from the 8 x 10½-inch letterhead to 8½ x 11-inch letterhead. The *business or standard* size letterhead is the most commonly used size for business correspondence.

Plain paper of the same size, quality, and color should be used for the second and succeeding pages of longer letters.

Plain Paper

8.3 Varying qualities of plain paper are available for office tasks. A good quality of bond paper should be used for reports, tables, outlines, and other similar items that are distributed to others, are relatively permanent, or will be referred to in the future. A lesser quality of paper can be used for first-draft materials that are to be corrected or revised before the final typing.

Carbon Paper

8.4 Carbon paper comes in varying weights, from 4 to 10 pounds. The quality chosen depends on the number of copies to be made at one time and the number of times the carbon paper is to be used. Since copies are made of almost everything typed in the office and carbon paper is reusable, a good quality of carbon paper should be selected.

Copy Paper

8.5 Copy paper for carbon copies of correspondence is usually much thinner than paper used for originals. Copy paper is often referred to as *onionskin* or *manifold* paper. Copy paper may have the word "Copy" superimposed on it or may be colored for easy recognition in the files.

PROOFREADING

8.6 Proofreading is an essential skill for all office personnel, especially those who prepare typed correspondence and documents. The following steps will help ensure the accuracy of typed material:

1. Review any special instructions for preparing the material. Be sure they have been carried out.
2. Decide whether the material is properly placed on the page or form in an attractive manner.
3. Look over the typed item for obvious omissions or errors.

4. Read the entire item for *understanding*. This involves more than just reading each individual word. Read for *meaning*.
5. If the item contains unfamiliar content or technical matter, ask a co-worker to help. The typist should read from the original, the co-worker should follow the typewritten copy.
6. Double check names, figures, addresses, amounts, and dates to be sure they are accurate.
7. Proofread again line by line, checking the typed copy against the original.

CORRECTING

8.7 If extensive corrections must be made on a page of copy, it may be best to retype the entire page. If so, retype from the original document, not from the typed copy containing the errors.

Simple corrections may be made by erasing or by using correction liquids, correction paper, correction tape, or a correcting typewriter.

Erasing

8.8 Good erasing requires the use of an eraser, an erasing guide (a metal or plastic plate with various sizes and shapes of openings), and an erasing shield (a solid metal or plastic plate or a 3 × 5 card). Use a typing or ink eraser for originals and a soft eraser for carbon copies. Follow these steps in making corrections with an eraser:

1. Move the carriage to the extreme left or right so the eraser crumbs will not fall into the machine.
2. Raise the paper bail and roll the paper forward or backward to get to the error easily.
3. Place the erasing shield between the original and the first carbon copy, in front of the carbon paper, to protect the copies from being smudged as you make the correction on the original.
4. Place the erasing guide over the error, using the appropriate opening in the guide. This will enable you to erase only the incorrect letter without smudging adjacent letters. Erase the original one letter at a time using short, vertical movements. Brush or blow the eraser crumbs from the paper.
5. Insert the erasing shield between the first and second carbon copies, in front of the second carbon sheet. Make the correction on the first carbon copy, using a *soft* eraser.
6. Repeat step 5 for each remaining carbon copy, proceeding from front to back in the pack.
7. Return the paper to the correct line of writing. Be sure to check the alignment before typing the correction.

Correction Liquid

8.9   Correction liquid can be used to block out incorrect letters, words, or lines in typed copy. When the appearance of the original is especially important, correction liquid should probably not be used, because correction liquid is generally easy to see. If the original material is to be photocopied, corrections can be made with correction liquid since the corrections will not be visible on the photocopies. The following steps are recommended when using correction liquid:

1. Position the paper so that the error is accessible.
2. Shake the bottle well before using.
3. Apply the liquid sparingly. Touch it on, do not brush it on. (Brushing causes the ink from the ribbon to smear.)
4. Allow the liquid to dry thoroughly before typing over it.
5. Be sure to close the top of the bottle tightly after using.

Correction liquid can be purchased in various colors to match the stationery being used.

Correction Paper

8.10   Correction paper is available in small rolls or squares. It is a chalk-backed paper that can be used to make corrections on both originals and carbon copies. The corrections are not permanent and are usually easy to see. However, they may be acceptable when speed and ease of correction are more important than appearance. To be least noticeable, correction paper should be used only when the retyped letters are of the same size and shape as the incorrect letters. The following steps are recommended when using correction paper:

1. Move the carriage to the error.
2. Place the piece of correction paper over the error, chalky side against the typed copy. (Make sure that the correction paper is between the ribbon and the paper.)
3. Retype the *incorrect* letter to cover it with the chalky coating.
4. Remove the correction paper; check to see if the incorrect letter has been completely covered.
5. Backspace to the error and type the *correct* letter. Retype if necessary to get a good impression.

Correction Tape

8.11   Correction tape is available in self-sticking strips. These strips may be used to cover whole words, lines, or paragraphs. A strip of tape the same length as the error is cut and removed from the backing paper.

It is then placed *over* the error. Corrections can be typed directly on the tape. Correction tape is quite visible and should probably be used only when the original is to be photocopied.

Correcting Typewriter

8.12 Some modern typewriter models have a special correcting ribbon that when engaged allows the typist to "lift-off" the error from the page before the correct letter is typed. On some models, the correcting ribbon is part of the typing ribbon. In this instance, the ribbon deposits a "white-out" material on top of the error. On other models, the typewriter ribbon, in a cartridge pack, must be completely removed and replaced by a "white-out" type of correction ribbon, also in a cartridge pack. The following steps are generally used on correcting typewriters:

1. If necessary, insert or engage the correcting ribbon.
2. Depress the backspace-correction key on the typewriter.
3. Retype the incorrect letter.
4. Type the correct letter.
5. If necessary, remove or disengage the correcting ribbon.

Squeezing Letters

8.13 If an error has been made in a word by omitting a letter, the word can be corrected by "squeezing" the omitted letter within the space. This eliminates having to retype the entire line or the entire item. To squeeze a letter into the space, use the following method:

1. Remove the incorrect word from the copy by erasing or using correction liquid or correction paper.
2. Move the typewriter carriage to the space *before* the first letter of the word to be corrected.
3. On manual typewriters, hold down the space bar while you type the first letter of the word. On electric typewriters, use the half-space key (if available) or position the carriage for the half space manually.
4. Repeat this procedure for the remaining letters in the word. The word should be squeezed into the original space.

```
the generl atmosphere

the general atmosphere
```

Spreading Letters

8.14 If an error has been made in a word by putting in too many letters, the word can be retyped in the same space by "spreading" the letters. Use the following steps to spread a word:

1. Remove the incorrect word from the copy by erasing or using correction liquid or correction paper.
2. Move the typewriter carriage to the position of the *first* letter in the word.
3. On manual typewriters, hold down the space bar while you type the first letter of the word. On electric typewriters, use the half-space key (if available) or position the carriage manually for the half space.
4. Repeat this procedure for the remaining letters of the word. The word should be spread out in the original space.

the generral atmosphere

the general atmosphere

MAKING CARBON COPIES

8.15 The use of carbon paper to make copies of typed materials is still the most common method used. However, photocopying is becoming more and more important in the modern office. Materials can also be duplicated using a variety of other processes and methods. The method used depends on the quantity to be duplicated, the equipment and skill available, and the desired quality of the copies.

Using Carbon Paper

8.16 As many as ten copies of an item can be made using carbon paper. Care should be maintained while assembling and using the carbon pack—the original, the copy paper, and the carbon paper. Since carbon copies are used as file copies and for distribution to others, it is important that they be neat and legible.

8.17 Assemble and insert the carbon pack into the typewriter as follows:

1. To assemble the carbon pack, lay the copy paper flat on the desk. Place a sheet of carbon paper, dull (inky or carbon) side down on top of the sheet of copy paper. Place as many sets of copy paper and carbon paper as required to top of the first set. Finally, place the letterhead or original sheet of paper on top.

2. Lift the carbon pack, and turn it so the dull (inky or carbon) side of the carbon paper faces you. Straighten all the edges of the carbon pack by gently tapping them on the desk.
3. Disengage the paper release. Drop the carbon pack into the typewriter and insert it into position.
4. As the carbon pack begins to appear in front of the cylinder, engage the paper release. The carbon pack is now ready for use.

If the carbon pack is thick and unmanageable, place the top edge of the carbon pack under the flap of a large envelope before inserting into the typewriter. Remove the envelope after the pack is in the typewriter. Disengage and engage the paper release a time or two, releasing the tension, to avoid wrinkling the carbon paper.

Before beginning to type, check the position of all carbon sheets to be sure the dull side is facing away from you.

Always disengage the paper release before removing the carbon pack from the typewriter. Remove the carbon paper between the sheets with care. Carbon paper is usually longer than letterhead stationery or plain paper. You can remove the carbon paper by holding the carbon pack in one upper corner while you pull all the carbon sheets from the bottom. Handle the carbon paper carefully to ensure that the copies do not become smudged or fingerprinted. Do not attempt to use carbon paper beyond its normal life or illegible copies will result.

Carbon Sets

8.18 Carbon sets, made of a one-use sheet of carbon paper lightly glued to a sheet of copy paper, are used in many offices. They make assembling carbon sets much simpler for the typist and are easier to work with. The carbon sheets are disposed of after being used one time.

MAKING PHOTOCOPIES

8.19 Many firms today make photocopies of items prepared in the office. Machines available today can make few or many copies, in one or more colors, and may also provide collated sets. Some machines can copy on both sides of the paper. Others can reduce the size of the original copy. Some can even copy full-color documents or make duplicating masters and transparencies. While somewhat more expensive to make than carbon copies, the process is much faster and, therefore, may be less expensive per copy when many copies are needed. Most of the machines are simple to operate and require only a short training session or reading of the manufacturer's instructions.

DUPLICATING

Some offices utilize duplicating equipment to make quantities of copies—from 10 to 10,000. The three most common methods of duplicating are offset or multilith duplicating, stencil or mimeograph duplicating, and spirit or fluid duplicating.

Offset or Multilith Duplicating

8.20 Offset masters, made of a specially coated paper, can duplicate several thousand professional-quality copies on an offset or multilith machine. Follow these steps in preparing an offset master:

1. Be careful about touching the paper. Its special coating can be spoiled by fingerprints.
2. Make sure the keys are clean and that the typewriter is equipped with an offset or carbon ribbon.
3. Insert the master into the typewriter so the white surface faces you. Type the copy on the master.
4. To make corrections on the master, erase lightly with an ordinary eraser or an offset eraser. Type the correction.

Operating an offset duplicator requires special training. The copies are of much higher quality than those from other duplicating methods; however, the cost of supplies and maintenance is greater.

By using various colors of ink, a competent offset operator can add variety to the appearance. Offset masters can be stored and reused for additional copies.

Stencil or Mimeograph Duplicating

8.21 A mimeograph stencil, made of a waxy sheet attached to a backing sheet, can duplicate up to one thousand copies on a mimeograph machine. Follow these steps in preparing the stencil:

1. Be sure the typewriter type is clean. Since the type bars will, in effect, "cut through" the waxy sheet, the keys must be clean so that the impressions will be clear.
2. Set the ribbon indicator at the stencil position. The keys will strike the waxy sheet directly without going through the typewriter ribbon.
3. Read the instructions to see if the cushion sheet is needed between the waxy sheet and the backing sheet. If not, remove it.
4. Insert the set into the typewriter. The waxy sheet should face you. Type the copy on the sheet.

5. To make corrections, gently rub the error on the waxy sheet with a paper clip or glass rod to close the wax over the error. Apply a thin coat of stencil correction fluid with a brush and let dry thoroughly. Type the correction with a light touch.

After typing, the waxy sheet is detached from the backing sheet and fastened to the drum of the mimeograph machine. Ink flows through the impressions cut in the waxy sheet onto the copy paper.

Electric typewriters, because they have a firm, even stroke, generally prepare better stencils than manual typewriters.

Handwriting and designs can be applied to stencils using special writing instruments (called *styli*) and materials such as patterns and screens.

Electronic stencil makers are available, which can transfer the original copy directly to the stencil without typing.

If stencils are to be reused, they should be stored flat between sheets of absorbent paper in a cool, dry place.

Spirit or Fluid Duplicating

8.22 Spirit or fluid duplicating is not widely used in business offices. It is, however, used frequently in schools and in religious organizations.

Prepare a spirit master, made of a carbon-coated sheet attached to a sheet of white paper, for use on the spirit duplicator as follows:

1. Remove the protective sheet between the white sheet and the carbon-coated sheet.
2. Insert the set into the typewriter so the white sheet is toward you. Type the copy on the white sheet. The carbon is transferred to the back of the white sheet.
3. To make corrections, gently scrape the error from the *back of the white sheet* with a sharp knife or razor blade. Place a small piece of the carbon-coated sheet (cut from a corner) over the error on the carbon-coated sheet and retype the correct letter or word. Be sure to remove the piece used to correct the error before continuing.

   Whole words, lines, and paragraphs can be deleted from the white sheet by covering the deletion (on the back of the white sheet) with a piece of transparent tape. You cannot retype over the deletion since the transparent tape will not hold the carbon coating.

After typing, separate the white sheet from the carbon-coated sheet and attach it to the drum of the spirit duplicator. Up to a maximum of about three hundred copies can be made from one master.

In the spirit duplicating process, a special fluid combines with the carbon on the white sheet and transfers a small amount of that carbon onto the copy paper. Carbon masters generally come in black or purple, although other colors are available. Since the special fluid transfers the carbon already on the white sheet, several colors can be used on one master.

CHAIN FEEDING ENVELOPES AND CARDS

8.23 When a large number of cards or envelopes are to be typed, a system known as *chain feeding* can be used to speed up the process. Proceed as follows for "front feeding" envelopes:

1. Stack the envelopes at the side of the typewriter.
2. Insert the first envelope into the typewriter in typing position.
3. Type the first envelope. Roll the envelope back until about $\frac{1}{2}$ inch remains visible.
4. Insert the second envelope in the front between the first envelope and the platen or cylinder.
5. Turn the cylinder back to remove the first envelope. Position the second envelope in typing position.
6. Continue this process, dropping an envelope in the front of the typewriter as you remove each typed envelope.

8.24 Proceed as follows for "back feeding" envelopes:

1. Stack the envelopes at the side of the typewriter.
2. Insert the first envelope into the typewriter in typing position.
3. Place the second envelope into the back of the typewriter.
4. Type the first envelope. Turn the cylinder forward to remove the first envelope and, at the same time, insert a third envelope into the back of the typewriter. The second envelope will move into typing position as you do this.
5. Continue this process, dropping an envelope into the back of the typewriter as you remove each typed envelope.

Cards can also be typed rapidly using this method.

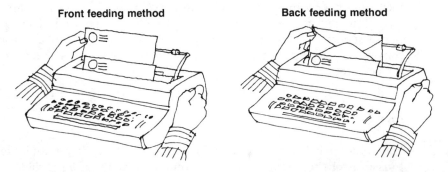

Front feeding method   Back feeding method

Figure 8-3

COMMONLY TYPED BUSINESS ITEMS

The most commonly typed items in an office include: agendas, cards, envelopes, file folder labels, graphs, interoffice memos, invoices, itineraries, letters, minutes, news releases, purchase orders, reports, and tables.

Agenda

8.25 An agenda (see Figure 8-4) is a listing of subjects to be covered in a meeting. Agendas, usually prepared by the person in charge of the meeting, are distributed to those who will attend. By receiving the agenda prior to the meeting, the participants are able to study the items and prepare for the discussion.

Cards

8.26 Cards (see Figure 8-5) are most frequently used to keep records of names and addresses. They may be prepared for employees, customers, and others.

Envelopes

8.27 Envelopes of an appropriate size are prepared for all items to be mailed. See Sections 8.23–8.24 and 9.31–9.35 for a discussion of envelopes and how they are prepared.

Expense Reports

8.28 Expense reports (see Figure 8-6) are itemized records of expenses incurred on a business trip. Daily expenses for lodging, meals, transportation, entertainment, and tips are generally required. The expense report may also include information on destinations and the purpose of the trip. Receipts must often accompany expense reports for verification.

File Folder Labels

8.29 File folder labels (see Figure 8-7) generally come in gummed or pressure-sensitive strips, which are then attached to the file folders. Labels come in a variety of sizes, shapes, and colors.

Graphs

8.30 Graphs are often prepared to illustrate facts and figures in reports. Figures 8-8 to 8-10 are examples of a bar graph, a line graph, and a circle graph.

Interoffice Memorandums

8.31 Interoffice memos are used to carry on correspondence within the company. See Sections 9.36–9.37 for a discussion and examples of half-page and full-page memos.

Invoices

8.32 Invoices (see Figure 8-11), generally in multiple copies, are prepared to include the details of a sale. They are actually bills or statements and are often sent with or immediately after the shipment of the goods ordered.

Itineraries

8.33 An itinerary (see Figure 8-12) is a listing of the dates, appointments, accommodations, and methods of travel to be used in a trip. In addition to all the needed information, an itinerary may contain special notes or reminders for the traveler. An original is prepared for the traveler and copies may also be prepared for those who may need to get in touch with the traveler.

Letters

8.34 A discussion and examples of business letters are found in Sections 9.1–9.29.

8.35 Minutes (see Figure 8-13) of meetings are generally prepared to indicate who attended, what discussions were held, and what decisions were reached. The original becomes the permanent record of the meeting; copies are usually prepared for all those who attended.

News Release

8.36 News releases (see Figure 8-14) are prepared on special news release forms to present information for publication or other use by the news media.

Purchase Orders

8.37 Purchase orders (see Figure 8-15) are prepared in multiple copies to order merchandise from outside-the-company suppliers. They serve as written records of all purchases made.

Purchase Requisitions

8.38 Purchase requisitions (see Figure 8-16) are used to order certain office supplies and equipment. They are usually sent to one person who coordinates all purchasing activities for the firm. Purchase requisitions are generally prepared before a purchase order can be completed.

Reports

8.39 Reports, both formal and informal, present information that is gathered for a specific purpose. A complete discussion and examples of reports are found in Sections 10.1–10.35.

Tables

8.40 Tables of various kinds are used to report information, generally of a statistical nature. Examples of tables and how to prepare them are found in Sections 10.36–10.39.

Voucher Checks

8.41 Voucher checks (see Figure 8-17) are checks with attached stubs. The stubs are used to show the reasons for the check preparation. They are detached before cashing and may be kept as a record of receipt.

```
                    AGENDA FOR MONTHLY STAFF MEETING
                       Tuesday, February 12, 1980
                       9 a.m. in the Conference Room

       The following items will be considered at the meeting:

       1.  Welcome new employees

       2.  The sales conference program

       3.  Fourth quarter sales report

       4.  Exhibit booth at sales conference

       5.  Report on status of consideration of opening new branch office
```

Figure 8-4   Agenda

QUEEN CITY NEWS

Queen City News
7023 Beechmont Avenue
Cincinnati, OH 45230

Figure 8-5   Card

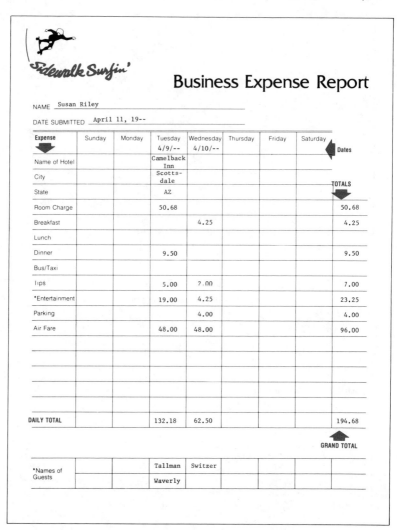

Business Expense Report

NAME Susan Riley

DATE SUBMITTED April 11, 19--

Expense	Sunday	Monday	Tuesday 4/9/--	Wednesday 4/10/--	Thursday	Friday	Saturday	TOTALS
Name of Hotel			Camelback Inn					
City			Scotts-dale					
State			AZ					
Room Charge			50.68					50.68
Breakfast				4.25				4.25
Lunch								
Dinner			9.50					9.50
Bus/Taxi								
Tips			5.00	2.00				7.00
*Entertainment			19.00	4.25				23.25
Parking				4.00				4.00
Air Fare			48.00	48.00				96.00
DAILY TOTAL			132.18	62.50				194.68

GRAND TOTAL

*Names of Guests			Tallman	Switzer				
			Waverly					

Figure 8-6   Expense report

QUEEN CITY NEWS
Cincinnati, OH 45230

AUDREY'S OFFICE SUPPLIES
Jackson, MS 39531

Figure 8-7   File folder labels

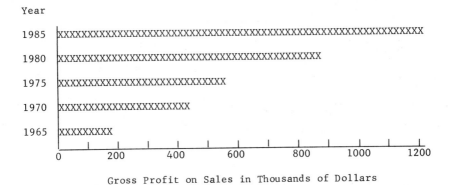

ANDERSON HILLS MFG. CO.
Gross Profit on Sales
1965-1985 (Projected)

Gross Profit on Sales in Thousands of Dollars

Figure 8-8   Bar graph

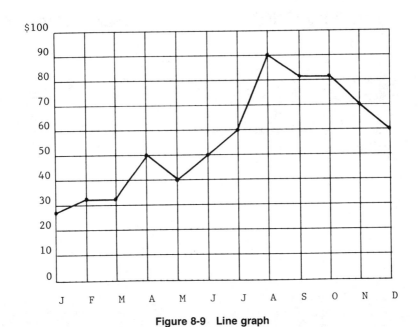

DILLON SUPPLY COMPANY
1980 Net Sales (in Thousands)

Figure 8-9   Line graph

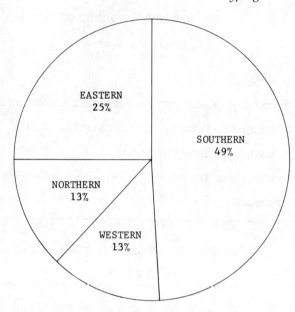

Figure 8-10   Circle graph

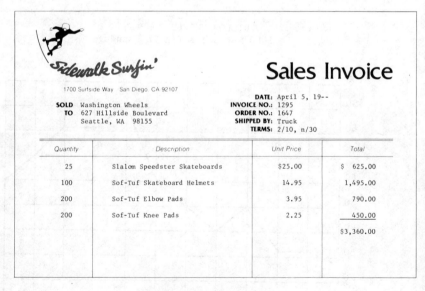

Figure 8-11   Invoice

```
                              ITINERARY OF SUSAN RILEY

                                 April 9-10, 19--

                                 Phoenix, Arizona

     Tuesday, April 9

       7:30 a.m.    Leave San Diego International Airport, American Flight 428

       9:27 a.m.    Arrive Phoenix Airport; Mr. Tallman to furnish transportation to
                    Phoenix office

      10:00 a.m.    Meet with Mr. James Taylor, Phoenix branch office manager, to
                    discuss new office procedures manual

      11:00 a.m.    Meet with Mr. John Titus, exhibit chairperson of the National
                    Invitational Skateboard Tournament, to discuss exhibit

      12:00 noon    Lunch with Mr. Tallman and Mr. Titus at Casa Grande Restaurant

       2:00 p.m.    Meet with Miss Toni Winkler, prospective sales representative

       4:00 p.m.    Meet with regional sales staff to present first quarter sales
                    report

       8:00 p.m.    Dinner with Mr. Tallman and Mr. Waverly, Regional Olympic Com-
                    mittee representative

                    Overnight accommodations at Camelback Inn, Scottsdale

     Wednesday, April 10

       9:00 a.m.    Breakfast meeting with Ms. Renee Switzer, chairperson of judges'
                    panel for National Invitational, Camelback Inn poolside restaurant

      11:45 a.m.    Leave for Phoenix Airport; Mr. Tallman to furnish transportation

      12:55 p.m.    Leave Phoenix, American Flight 525; lunch served on plane

       1:53 p.m.    Arrive San Diego
```

Figure 8-12 Itinerary

SUMMARY OF STAFF MEETING

TIME AND PLACE The monthly staff meeting of the management of Pleasure Island was held on Wednesday, May 17, 19--, in the International Room. The general manager, Kelly Ryan, presided.

ATTENDANCE Those in attendance were Marilyn Steiner, Raymond Zelinski, Harold Tyner, William Rhodes, Karen Whitesides, Allison Matthews, Samuel Browning, Craig Littlefield, Hans Anderson, Anthony Devine, Curtis Lockman, Patricia Cullen, Kelly Ryan, and Lynn Baldwin.

DISCUSSION Mr. Anderson presented the report of the Fourth of July Spectacular committee. Among the festivities planned are a parade of the Fantasyland characters, an air show, the appearance of Lilli Ramone and The Daltons, and a spectacular fireworks display.

Mr. Littlefield reported on negotiations to purchase a new ride, the "Indy 500," which utilizes a two-track system permitting patrons to "race" vehicles down a half-mile hard-surface track. Mr. Littlefield is to visit two sister theme parks, Treasure Island and Leisure Island, to evaluate their versions of this ride.

Ms. Matthews stated that contracts were being prepared for Lilli Ramone and The Daltons.

Mr. Devine reported that the new grooming standards for seasonal employees have been finalized and are to be included in the next revision of the handbook.

Mr. Ryan reported that a newsletter, The Passport, would begin soon.

Mrs. Steiner reported that plans had been made to honor the 50 millionth guest with a five-year pass, a special luncheon, and various gifts.

NEXT MEETING The date of the next staff meeting was set for Wednesday, June 14, in the Continental Room.

ADJOURNMENT The meeting was adjourned at 10:30 a.m.

Lynn Baldwin
Recorder

Figure 8-13 Minutes

News Release

7000 PLEASURE ISLAND DRIVE
NEW ORLEANS, LA 70189

To: <u>New Orleans Times Picayune</u>

For Release: IMMEDIATELY   **Contact:** Hans Anderson

50 MILLIONTH VISITOR RECOGNIZED

Mrs. Janice Wall, a senior citizen of Bogalusa, Louisiana, recently became the 50 millionth visitor to Pleasure Island. Mrs. Wall was honored with a five-year pass, a luncheon at the International Restaurant, and various gifts from Pleasure Island. Accompanied by her husband, Mrs. Wall said that she had been a frequent visitor to Pleasure Island, especially since her husband retired five years earlier.

Kelly Ryan, general manager of Pleasure Island, presented the awards to Mrs. Wall at the entrance to the park on Saturday, May 20. Mrs. Wall was part of a huge crowd of some 55,000 who visited the park that day.

The presentation was part of a year-long program by Pleasure Island to highlight the accomplishments of the park during its tenth year of operation.

# # #

Figure 8-14   News release

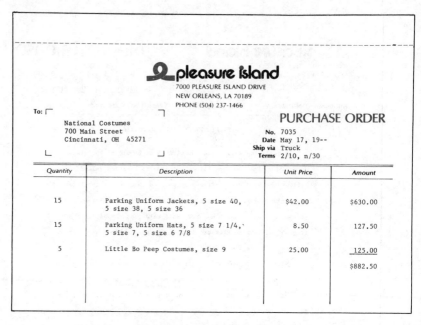

Figure 8-15   Purchase order

ANDERSON HILLS MFG. CO.   PURCHASE REQUISITION

Requisition No.   2516
Date Issued   April 3, 19--
Date Required   May 3, 19--

Deliver To   William Rhodes
Approved By   *Rmh*

Qty.	Cat. No.	Description	Cat. Price	Total
2	1614290	4 Drawer Filing Cabinet, Tan	$ 92.00	$184.00
5	2840066	Revolving Arm Chairs, Tan	61.99	309.95
5	4496311	Pedestal Office Desks, Tan	156.30	781.50

Suggested Vendor   Audrey's Office Supplies
301 W. Capitol Street
Jackson, MS 39531

Figure 8-16   Purchase requisition

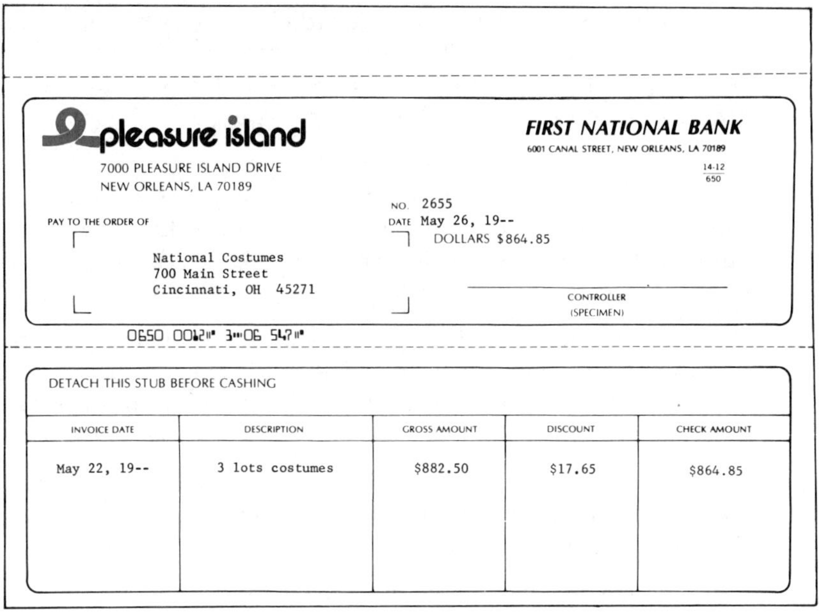

pleasure island
7000 PLEASURE ISLAND DRIVE
NEW ORLEANS, LA 70189

FIRST NATIONAL BANK
6001 CANAL STREET, NEW ORLEANS, LA 70189
14-12/650

NO. 2655
DATE May 26, 19--
PAY TO THE ORDER OF
DOLLARS $864.85

National Costumes
700 Main Street
Cincinnati, OH 45271

CONTROLLER
(SPECIMEN)

DETACH THIS STUB BEFORE CASHING

INVOICE DATE	DESCRIPTION	GROSS AMOUNT	DISCOUNT	CHECK AMOUNT
May 22, 19--	3 lots costumes	$882.50	$17.65	$864.85

Figure 8-17 Voucher check

TYPING TIPS AND SHORTCUTS

8.42 Arrange your desk for the most economical use of space, time, and motion. If you find that items are not conveniently located, do not hesitate to rearrange your desk.

Choose your typewriter eraser to match your paper. Use a hard typewriter eraser for high-quality bond. Use a soft eraser for softer bonds and carbon copies. An eraser with an edge will permit you to erase just one letter at a time.

When erasing carbon copies always use a card or a guard. An inexpensive card can be made from an old file folder or the cardboard backing of a used tablet.

A small (2″ × 2″) piece of sandpaper can be kept in the top drawer of your desk and used to clean off carbon which has accumulated on the eraser when erasing carbon copies.

When correcting mistakes in the last line of type, always turn the paper backwards in the typewriter until the mistake rests conveniently on the paper table where it can be easily erased.

When composing a letter, report, article, or other project, quickly type a rough draft copy. This will save time in having to write all of your thoughts out by hand. Corrections, additions, and rearranging can be done on the rough draft before typing a final copy.

You can easily make a useful page line guide. At the extreme right edge of a full sheet of paper, type the numbers 1 through 33 on consecutive lines, one number exactly under the one above. To number the lower half of the page, type 33 again. This time type a number on each subsequent line but work *backwards* from 33 to 1.

Using this guide as a backing sheet, position it behind each page so that the numbers appear to the right of the sheet of paper. You can automatically see where to start typing the first line and you can plan where to type the last line of the page and any footnotes.

To save time, number footnotes consecutively throughout a paper or report. Then type a list of footnotes on a separate page at the conclusion of the paper or report.

When typing above or below the line (as for sub- or superscripts) use the ratchet release lever. The platen can be revolved to any point. When the lever is engaged again, the platen will return to the same position at which you were typing originally.

When typing leaders, align them vertically by typing only on even or only on odd spaces.

When typing ruled tables, save time by drawing the ruled lines after the table has been removed from the typewriter. Using a ruler, draw all necessary lines with a pen of matching ink.

Drawing lines at the typewriter—

   To draw vertical lines at the typewriter, insert a pencil or pen in the notch or hole in the cardholder. Release the ratchet release lever and roll the platen up or down.

   To draw horizontal lines at the typewriter, insert a pencil or pen in the notch or one of the holes in the cardholder. Use the carriage release lever and move the carriage right or left as you draw a line.

To type labels or small cards do the following: Using a half-sheet of paper, make a horizontal pleat about $\frac{1}{2}$ to 1 inch deep going across the sheet of paper. Feed this sheet into the typewriter until the pleat is in typing position. Insert the label or small card. Adjust paper with pleat and label or card to typing position and type.

Indicate the bottom margin of reports, etc., by making a faint horizontal pencil mark at the point where the last line of the page is to be typed. When this line appears in typing position, erase the line and type your last line of type before starting the next page.

NAME _____

Self-Check Exercise

SECTION I

From the list at the right, select the term that matches the statement at the left. Place the letter of the term in the blank to the left of the statement.

_____ 1. Used by executives for private correspondence

_____ 2. A type of paper used for making copies

_____ 3. A plastic or metal plate with various sizes and shapes of openings

_____ 4. One method of correcting incorrect letters or words

_____ 5. A technique used to place a word in a space slightly smaller than the word ordinarily requires

_____ 6. A sheet of one-use carbon paper attached to a sheet of copy paper

_____ 7. A method of duplicating that uses a carbon-coated sheet attached to a white sheet

_____ 8. A method of duplicating in which the ink flows through openings cut into a waxy sheet onto the copy paper

_____ 9. A method of duplicating that produces professional-quality copies but that requires specialized training

_____10. A system used to speed the process of typing a large number of envelopes or cards

A. Carbon set

B. Chain feeding

C. Correction liquid

D. Erasing guide

E. Executive letterhead

F. Manifold

G. Offset duplicating

H. Spirit duplicating

I. Squeezing

J. Stencil duplicating

SECTION II

Fill in the blanks below with the appropriate terms.

1. A(n) _____ is a listing of items to be discussed in a meeting.

2. _____ are used for communications within the company.

3. The _____ of a meeting indicate who attended, what discussions were held, and what decisions were reached.

117

4. A(n) _____ presents information for publication or use by the media.

5. A(n) _____ is a listing of dates, appointments, accommodations, and methods of travel to be used in a trip.

6. A(n) _____ graph, _____ graph, or_____ graph may be used to illustrate facts or figures in a graphic manner in reports.

7. _____ are prepared in multiple copies to include the details of a sale.

8. A(n) _____ is prepared when merchandise is to be ordered from outside-the-company suppliers.

9. A(n) _____ has a feature that allows the typist to "lift off" an incorrect letter.

10. The procedure for carefully studying typed material to be sure that it is accurate is called _____.

Check your answers in the back of the book.

9 Business Letters and Office Communications

LETTERS are the lifeblood of business. They introduce people, make sales, order products and services, inform customers, correct errors, persuade buyers, make inquiries, and perform a host of other functions. They represent the company to those receiving the letters.

First impressions—good and bad—are created by business letters. A good first impression will be made if the letter is arranged so that it is pleasing to the eye, if the parts are correctly placed, if there are no errors in spelling and punctuation, if it is clean and free of smudges and fingerprints, and if the typing is strong and clear.

The cost of producing a business letter has risen rapidly in the last few years until it is rather sizable today. Because most businesses produce many letters each day, it is important that each letter be produced quickly, without errors, and in a manner that will do the intended job while representing the company appropriately.

9

LETTERS

9.1 Business letters may contain as many as 18 parts. An asterisk in the following list denotes those parts found in most business letters.

*1. Printed letterhead   10. Company name
*2. Date   *11. Signature
 3. Mailing notation   *12. Typed name
*4. Inside address   *13. Title
 5. Attention line   *14. Reference initials
*6. Salutation   15. Enclosure notation
 7. Subject line   16. Separate cover notation
*8. Body   17. Copy notation
*9. Complimentary close   18. Postscript

These letter parts are shown in Figure 9-1.

Figure 9-1   Business letter

Letter Placement

9.2 In order to place a letter on a page attractively, you may use the following chart to determine line lengths, date position, and spacing between the date and inside address.

Length	No. of Words	Side Margins	Margin Settings Pica	Elite	Date Position (Line)	Lines between Date and Inside Address
Short	Under 100	2 inches	20-70	24-83	20	3
Medium	100-200	1½ inches	15-75	18-89	16-18	3
Long	201-300	1 inch	10-80	12-95	12-14	3
Two-page	Over 300	1 inch	10-80	12-95	12-14	3

If your company prefers to use a standard line length for all correspondence, you can obtain letter balance by adjusting the spaces between the letterhead and date. If necessary, make additional adjustments between the closing parts of the letter. With practice and experience, you can ensure proper balance without referring to letter placement tables.

LETTER PARTS

Letterhead

9.3 The printed letterhead (see part 1, Figure 9-1) usually contains the complete name and address of the company. It may also contain a telephone number, company insignia or logo, slogan, or other information.

If a business letter is written on plain paper, the address of the sender should be shown in place of the printed letterhead. This address, known as the *return address*, includes the sender's street address, city, state, and ZIP Code. The date appears immediately below the return address. The return address and date may be typed at the left margin, right margin, or centered, depending on the letter style.

Date

9.4 The date (see part 2, Figure 9-1) tells when the letter was typed and serves as a reference if several letters have been sent to or received from the same person or company. Keep the following points in mind:

1. Always type the date in full for regular business correspondence.

   ```
   May 13, 1980
   ```

   In military correspondence (and instances where this style has been adopted), the day of the month precedes the month and the year. There is no punctuation between the month and year.

   ```
   13 May 1980
   ```

2. Depending on the letter style and the placement of the letterhead, the date may be typed at the center of the page, at the right margin, balanced with the printed letterhead, or at the left margin.
3. Leave two to six lines between the date and the letterhead, depending on company practice and the design of the letterhead.

Mailing Notation

9.5 If the letter is to be sent via a special postal service (registered mail, certified mail, special delivery, etc.), a mailing notation (see part 3, Figure 9-1) should be typed at the left margin in all capital letters, a double space below the date.

Inside Address

9.6 The inside address (see part 4, Figure 9-1) is the complete name and address of the addressee, the individual or firm receiving the letter. The following points should be observed:

1. Type the inside address at the left margin. (See the placement chart in Section 9.2.)
2. Type the name of the person or company receiving the letter.
3. When a person's name includes an official title, type the title on the same line as the name or on the line following to maintain proper balance of the lines.
4. Spell out street names using numbers less than ten. Use figures for numbers over ten. Always spell out a compass point (north, south, east, west) that is part of the street name.

```
1337 Sixth Street
1337 North 161st Street
```

5. Always use figures for building numbers, with the exception of "One." Separate adjacent building and street numbers with a hyphen.

```
One Beacon Street
1337 - 161st Street
```

6. The complete name of the city, state, and ZIP Code must be shown. Use the two-letter state abbreviations recommended by the Postal Service. (See Section 4.5 for a list of these two-letter state abbreviations.) The ZIP Code must follow the two-letter abbreviation, separated by one space.

```
Ms. Elaine Washington    Miss Ruth Greenley
1327 Wilmington Drive    5031 West 16th Street
Jackson, MS 39207        Dover, IL 61323

Mr. Robert Hershey, Director
Social Clubs of America
148 Haywood Boulevard
San Diego, CA 92123
```

Attention Line

9.7 An attention line (see part 5, Figure 9-1) directs the letter to a specific person or department not named in the inside address. It is typed a double space below the inside address. It generally begins at the left margin, but it may be centered.

```
General Products, Inc.
8000 Capitol Drive
Colorado Springs, CO 80901

Attention: Mr. Kyle Tallman


Center Plaza Development
1647 Center Plaza
Topeka, KS 66604

            Attention Personnel Director
```

Salutation

9.8 Type the salutation (see part 6, Figure 9-1) at the left margin, a double space below the last line of the inside address or an attention line.

If open punctuation is used in the letter, no punctuation mark follows the salutation. If mixed punctuation is used, a colon follows the salutation.

```
Ms. Maria Malendez        Dr. James Moore
7105 Clearview Drive      Clearview Medical Center
Provo, UT 84601           Clearview, IA 51014

Dear Ms. Malendez         Dear Dr. Moore:
```

9.9 Depending on the relationship of the sender and the receiver of the letter, the salutation may range from informal to formal. The following salutations are arranged from informal to formal.

```
Dear Ted, Dear Dorothy
My dear Ted, My dear Dorothy
Dear Mr. Wilson, Dear Ms. Havlicek
My dear Mr. Wilson, My dear Ms. Havlicek
Dear Sir, Dear Madam
Sir, Madam
```

The following salutations are commonly used for business letters. (See Section 9.30 for other forms of address.)

To a business firm:	Gentlemen
	Ladies and Gentlemen
To an individual:	Dear Sir, Dear Madam
	Dear Miss, Mr., Mrs.,
	Ms. Goldstein
To a husband and wife:	Dear Mr. and Mrs. Chung
To two men:	Dear Mr. Jackson and
	Mr. Lesneski
	Dear Messrs. Gray and
	Turner
To two married women:	Dear Mrs. Phillips and
	Mrs. Dow
	Dear Mmes. Thames and
	Williams
To two single women:	Dear Miss Johnson and
	Miss Littlefield
	Dear Misses Tatum and Caryl
To two women, regardless	Dear Ms. Wayne and
of marital status:	Ms. Sanchez

In the AMS Simplified letter style (Figure 9-5), the salutation is omitted.

Subject Line

9.10 The emphasis of the letter may be highlighted by a subject line (see part 7, Figure 9-1). It is typed a double space below the salutation and may be centered, begun at the left margin, or begun at the paragraph point.

The word "Subject" may be used; however, the trend seems to be away from this practice. The subject line may be typed in all capital letters or in capitals and lowercase letters; it may or may not be underlined.

```
Dear Mr. Williams

          NATIONAL ADVERTISING CAMPAIGN

Dear Mr. Williams

National Advertising Campaign

Dear Mr. Williams

     Subject: National Advertising Campaign
```

Body

9.11 The body (see part 8, Figure 9-1) is the actual message. It begins a double space below the salutation or subject line.

Single spacing is generally used for the body of the letter, except for very short letters. Double space between paragraphs to ensure ease of reading and proper division of the message. Keep the right margin as even as possible to display a pleasing appearance. Paragraphs may or may not be indented, depending on the letter style used. Paragraph indentions are usually a uniform five spaces.

9.12 If two or more pages are required for the letter, type all pages after the first on plain stationery of the same quality and color as the first page. A heading should appear on all pages after the first in order to identify the pages easily. Two heading styles are shown below. Each heading begins 1 inch from the top of the page. Leave three blank lines between the heading and the continuation of the body.

```
BLOCK STYLE
Mrs. Alma Smith
Page 2
July 13, 1980
```

```
SPREAD STYLE
Mrs. Alma Smith            2            July 13, 1980
```

The block style is easier to type and less time consuming.

Complimentary Close

9.13 Type the complimentary close (see part 9, Figure 9-1) a double space below the last line of the body. It should align vertically with the typed date. Capitalize only the first word of the complimentary close.

If mixed punctuation is used, the complimentary close is followed by a comma; if open punctuation is used, no punctuation follows it.

9.14 The tone of the complimentary close should match that of the salutation. Typical complimentary closes, generally arranged from informal to formal, are as follows:

```
Cordially            Yours truly
Cordially yours      Yours very truly
Yours cordially      Very truly yours
Sincerely            Yours respectfully
Yours sincerely      Respectfully
Sincerely yours
```

Company name

9.15 Some companies follow the practice of typing the company name (see part 10, Figure 9-1) in all capital letters a double space below the complimentary close.

Sincerely yours

CENTRAL TRUST COMPANY

Since the company name already appears in the letterhead, this practice is really not necessary.

Signature

9.16 Leave enough space for the sender's signature (see part 11, Figure 9-1). Ordinarily, three blank lines are sufficient. However, more space may be needed to provide better balance for the letter on the page or to give the writer more space.

Sincerely yours

Robert J. Jones
Robert J. Jones

Typed Name and Title

9.17 Type the sender's name four or five lines below the complimentary close or a typed company name. The sender's official title may be typed on the same line as the name, separated by a comma. The title may also be typed on a separate line below the typed name (see parts 12 and 13, Figure 9-1).

Yours truly,

ACME RESEARCH, INC.

Paul R. Fischer
Paul R. Fisher, Manager

OR

Yours truly

Paul R. Fischer
Paul R. Fisher
Manager

9.18 The personal title of a man (Mr.) or the professional title of a man or a woman (Dr., Prof., etc.) should not appear before the typed signature. The personal title of a woman (Miss, Ms., Mrs.) may be shown in parentheses before the typed name. The signature of an unmarried woman may appear as follows:

Yours sincerely   Yours sincerely

(Miss) Amy Rutherford OR   *Amy Rutherford*

(Miss) Amy Rutherford   Amy Rutherford

The signature of a married woman or widow may appear as follows:

Yours sincerely   Yours sincerely

Lisa J. Lopez OR   *(Mrs.) Lisa J. Lopez*

(Mrs.) Lisa J. Lopez   Lisa J. Lopez

Some women prefer to use *Ms.* as their title, whether they are married or unmarried.

Yours sincerely

Corrine Austin

(Ms.) Corrine Austin

A married woman may prefer to sign her legal name, followed by her husband's name in the typed signature line.

Yours sincerely

Jammy Williamson

(Mrs.) Randall A. Williamson

Often a letter is signed by someone other than the sender. When this happens, the signer's initials should appear below the signature.

Sincerely yours

Robert J. Brown JT

Robert J. Brown

9.19   Sometimes a letter may be written for someone else. This may be indicated as follows:

Sincerely yours

Tim Holder

Tim Holder
Secretary to Raymond Brown

Reference Initials

9.20 The reference initials (see part 14, Figure 9-1) indicate who typed the letter. Type reference initials at the left margin, a double space below the last line of the signature line.

Yours truly,

Cynthia Wong

Cynthia Wong
General Manager

rmh

There are various ways to type reference initials. If the sender's initials are shown with the typist's, the sender's initials appear first.

RMH	CWong:RMH
rmh	CW–rmh
CW:rmh	CW/rmh

Enclosure Notation

9.21 When there is a reference in the body of the letter to other papers enclosed in the same envelope, type an enclosure notation (see part 15, Figure 9-1) a double space below the reference initials. The enclosure notation is a reminder to the typist to insert the items in the envelope and to the addressee to check to see that they were received.

When only one item is enclosed, type the word "Enclosure." When more than one item is enclosed, the number of items may be indicated or listed separately.

Enclosure	Enc.
Enclosures	Encl.
Enclosures 3	Encs.
Catalogue	Encls.
Order blanks	
Price list	

Separate Cover Notation

9.22 When a letter refers to something sent in another envelope or package, type a separate cover notation (see part 16, Figure 9-1) a double space below the reference initials or an enclosure notation.

When only one item is sent, type the words "Separate Cover." When more than one item is sent, the number or a list of the items may be shown following the notation. The delivery method of the items may also be indicated.

```
Separate Cover            Separate Cover 3
Separate Cover--          Separate Cover--Catalogue
   Air Express               Price List
```

Copy Notation

9.23 When carbon copies or photocopies of a letter are to be sent to persons other than the addressee, the copy notation "cc" (meaning carbon copy) or "c" (meaning copy) is typed a double space below the last line of typing (see part 17, Figure 9-1).

If the copies are to be sent to individuals without the knowledge of the addressee, the notation "bcc" (blind carbon copy) or "bc" (blind copy) is used. Before removing the letter from the typewriter type the bcc or bc notation on a card or piece of paper inserted in front of the original. The recipient's names will appear on all copies, but *not* on the original of the letter.

```
cc Mr. Randall            bc Mr. Randall
Copy to Mr. Randall       bcc Miss Smith
                              Mrs. Whiting
```

Postscript

9.24 A postscript (see part 18, Figure 9-1) is a brief addition to a letter, generally emphasizing a special point, setting it apart from the body of the letter. A postscript may be shown with or without the initials "P.S." Type the postscript at the left margin, a double space below the last line of typing.

```
P.S. Don't forget to send your order by October 15
     to receive the special discount.
```

LETTER PUNCTUATION

9.25 There are two basic punctuation styles used in business letters—open and mixed. In open punctuation, there is no punctuation mark after the salutation or complimentary close. In mixed punctuation, there is a colon after the salutation and a comma after the complimentary close. (See Figures 9-2, 9-3, 9-4.)

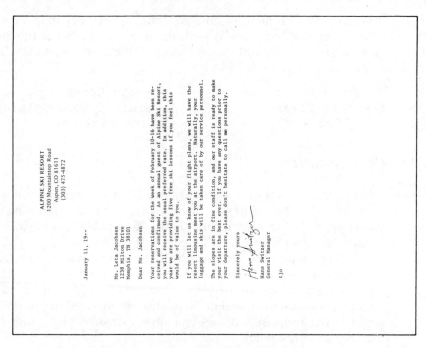

Figure 9-2   Block style letter, open punctuation

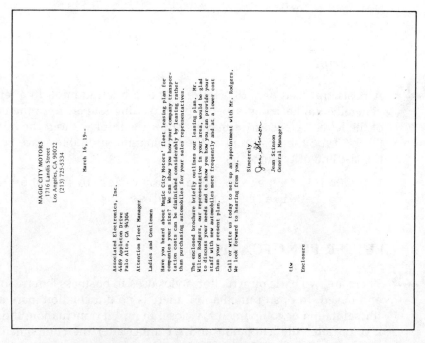

Figure 9-3   Modified block letter, blocked paragraphs, open punctuation

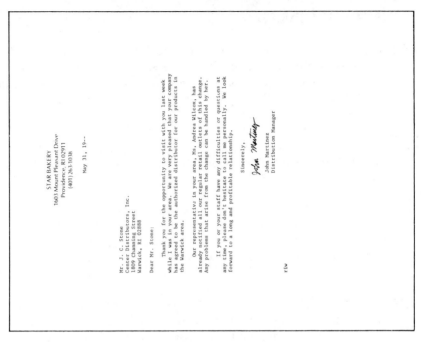

Figure 9-4   Modified block letter, indented paragraphs, mixed punctuation

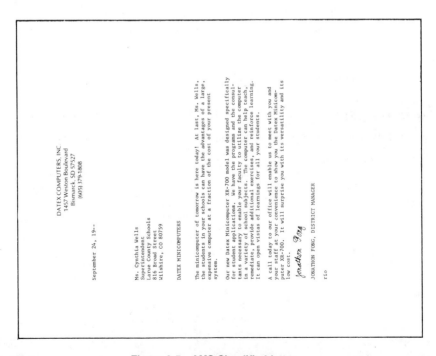

Figure 9-5   AMS Simplified letter

LETTER STYLES

9.26 There are several commonly used letter styles in business. Generally a firm uses only one style for all letters; however, practices do differ from firm to firm. The most common letter styles are block, modified block (with and without paragraph indentions), and the AMS Simplified style.

9.27 In the *block style* letter (Figure 9-2), all lines begin at the left margin. This modern letter style is easy to type since it requires no tabular stops.

9.28 In the *modified block style* letter (Figure 9-3 and 9-4), all lines begin at the left margin except the date and closing lines. The date and closing lines (complimentary close, company name, typed name, and official title) begin at the center. The paragraphs may or may not be indented, according to preference.

9.29 The *AMS Simplified style* letter (Figure 9-5) does not use a salutation or complimentary close. All lines begin at the left margin. A subject line is generally used, with a triple space before and after. Leave five to six blank lines between the last line of the body and the typed signature.

This letter, promoted by the American Management Society, is said to be the easiest to type, thus resulting in higher productivity.

FORMS OF ADDRESS

9.30 The correct forms of address for various officials are shown below.

Official and Address	Salutation	Complimentary Close
President of the United States		
The President	Sir, Madam	Very respectfully yours
The White House	Mr. President	Respectfully yours
Washington, DC 20500	Madam President	Respectfully
	Dear Mr. President	
	Dear Madam President	
Vice President of the United States		
The Vice President	Sir, Madam	Respectfully yours
The United States Senate	Dear Sir, Dear Madam	Very truly yours
Washington, DC 20510	Mr. Vice President	Sincerely yours
	Madam Vice President	
	Dear Mr. Vice President	
	Dear Madam Vice President	

Chief Justice

The Chief Justice	Sir, Madam	Respectfully
The Supreme Court of the	Mr. Chief Justice	Very truly yours
United States	Madam Chief Justice	Sincerely yours
Washington, DC 20543	Dear Mr. Chief Justice	
	Dear Madam Chief Justice	

Associate Justice

Mr., Mrs., Miss, Ms.	Sir, Madam	Very truly yours
Justice (Last name)	Mr. Justice	Sincerely yours
The Supreme Court of the	Madam Justice	
United States	Dear Mr. Justice	
Washington, DC 20543	Dear Madam Justice	

Cabinet Member

The Honorable (Full name)	Sir, Madam	Very truly yours
Secretary of (Department)	Dear Sir, Dear Madam	Sincerely yours
Washington, DC 20515	Dear Mr. Secretary	
	Dear Madam Secretary	

United States Senator

The Honorable (Full name)	Sir, Madam	Very truly yours
The United States Senate	Dear Sir, Dear Madam	Sincerely yours
Washington, DC 20510	Dear Senator (Last name)	

Congressional Representative

The Honorable (Full name)	Sir, Madam	Very truly yours
House of Representatives	Dear Sir, Dear Madam	Sincerely yours
Washington, DC 20515	Dear Representative (Last name)	
	Dear Congressman (Last name)	
	Dear Congresswoman (Last name)	

Governor of a State

The Honorable (Full name)	Sir, Madam	Respectfully yours
Governor of (State)	Dear Sir, Dear Madam	Very truly yours
(State capital, State, ZIP Code)	Dear Governor (Last name)	Sincerely yours

State Legislator

The Honorable (Full name)	Sir, Madam	Very truly yours
The House of Representatives (or The State Assembly)	Dear Sir, Dear Madam	Sincerely yours
(State capital, State, ZIP Code)	Dear Representative (Last name)	
	Dear Mr., Miss, Mrs., Ms. (Last name)	

State Senator

The Honorable (Full name)	Sir, Madam	Very truly yours
The State Senate	Dear Sir, Dear Madam	Sincerely yours
(State capital, State, ZIP Code)	Dear Senator (Last name)	

State Official

The Honorable (Last name)	Sir, Madam	Very truly yours
(Position)	Dear Sir, Dear Madam	Sincerely yours
(State capital, State, ZIP Code)	Dear Mr., Miss, Mrs., Ms. (Last name)	

Mayor

The Honorable (Full name)	Sir, Madam	Respectfully yours
Mayor of the City of (City)	Dear Sir, Dear Madam	Very truly yours
City Hall	Dear Mr. Mayor	Sincerely yours
(City, State, ZIP Code)	Dear Madam Mayor	
	Dear Mayor (Last name)	

ENVELOPES

9.31 There are two sizes of standard envelopes used most often in the office. The No. 10 envelope measures $9\frac{1}{2}$ x $4\frac{1}{8}$ inches and is used for one- and two-page letters and for letters with enclosures. Most companies use the No. 10 envelope for all general correspondence. The No. $6\frac{3}{4}$ envelope measures $6\frac{1}{2}$ x $3\frac{5}{8}$ inches and is generally used for small letterheads and may be used for one-page letters.

Envelopes should, of course, be the same quality, weight, finish, and color as the letterhead stationery.

9.32 The following should be remembered when preparing envelopes.

1. Be sure that the address on the envelope is the same as the inside address and that all names and addresses are accurate.
2. Type the address so that it will be attractively arranged and balanced. On a No. 10 envelope, begin the address $2\frac{1}{2}$ inches from the top edge of the envelope and 4 inches from the left edge. On a No. $6\frac{3}{4}$ envelope, begin the address 2 inches from the top edge and $2\frac{1}{2}$ inches from the left edge.
3. Single space the address. Type the city, state, and ZIP Code on the same line.

   To increase the speed and accuracy of mail delivery, the U.S. Postal System has recommended that addresses be typed in all capital letters with no punctuation. (See Figures 9-6 to 9-8).
4. Never use the word "City" in place of the actual name of the city.
5. If an attention line appears in the letter, it should also be typed on the envelope, immediately below the company name in the address. (See Figure 9-6.)

   Type special notations (such as "Please Forward," "Personal," and "Hold for Arrival") in all capital letters a double space below the return address.

   Type mailing notations (such as "Special Delivery" and "Registered Mail") in all capital letters below the position for the stamp.
6. Some firms follow the practice of typing the last name of the

sender immediately above the printed company name. This serves
as further identification

7. If a plain envelope is used, begin typing the return address in the
upper left corner two lines from the top and three spaces from the
left edge of the envelope.

Window envelopes are used primarily for sending statements to customers. When properly folded, the customer's name and address on
the statement appear in the "window" of the envelope.

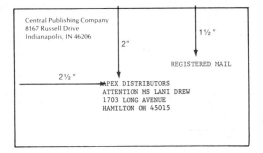

Figure 9-6   No. 6¾ envelope with notations

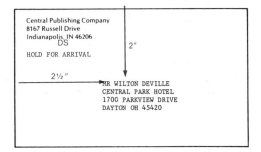

Figure 9-7   No. 6¾ envelope with notations

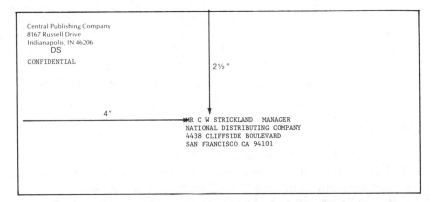

Figure 9-8   No. 10 envelope

FOLDING AND INSERTING LETTERS

9.33 To fold and insert a letter into a No. 10 envelope, follow these steps:

1. Place the letter on the desk face up.
2. Fold the bottom of the letter up, slightly less than one third of the way.
3. Fold the top of the letterhead down, leaving about $\frac{1}{2}$ inch.
4. Put the letter in the envelope, inserting the last crease first.

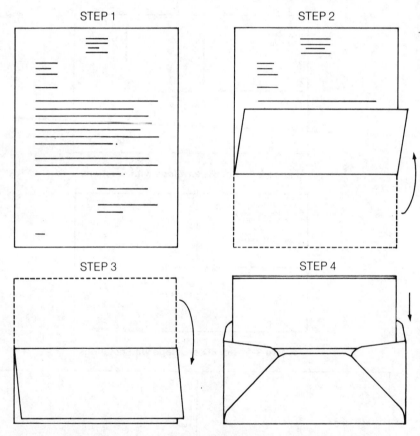

Figure 9-9   Folding and inserting letter into No. 10 envelope

9.34 To fold and insert a letter into a No. $6\frac{3}{4}$ envelope, follow these steps:

1. Place the letter on the desk face up.
2. Fold the bottom of the letter up to within $\frac{1}{2}$ inch of the top edge.
3. Fold from right to left about one third of the way.
4. Fold from left to right to within $\frac{1}{2}$ inch of the right side.
5. Put the letter in the envelope, inserting the last crease first.

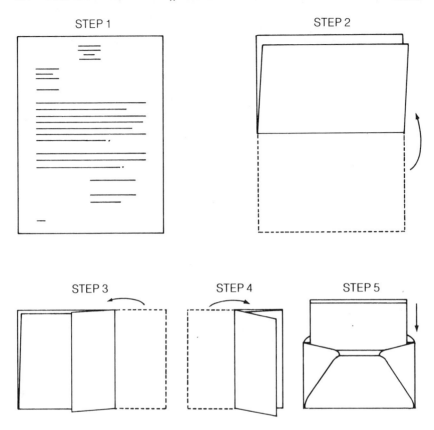

Figure 9-10   Folding and inserting letter into No. 6¾ envelope

9.35 To fold and insert a letter into a window envelope, follow these steps:

1. Place the letter on the desk face down, with the letterhead toward you.
2. Fold down, slightly less than one third of the way.
3. Fold up, making sure that the address is visible.
4. Put the letter in the envelope, inserting the last crease first. Make sure that the address is visible through the window.

To fold and insert a statement into a window envelope, follow these steps:

1. Place the form on the desk face down.
2. Fold the bottom half of the form up.
3. Put the form into the envelope, inserting the crease first. Make sure that the address is visible through the window.

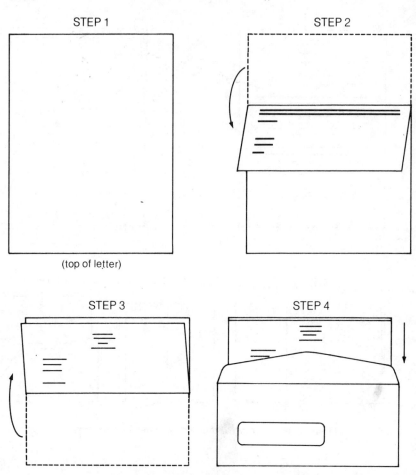

Figure 9-11   **Folding and inserting letter into window envelope**

INTEROFFICE MEMORANDUMS

9.36 Interoffice messages are generally typed on specially printed interoffice memorandum forms. These forms vary in size, color, and quality from regular office stationery. Because they are intended for circulation only within the office, the inside address, salutation, complimentary close, signature, and formal titles are generally omitted. The company name may or may not appear on the form. Even though the message is not formally signed, the sender generally initials it.

The memos may be printed on half-page forms for short messages or on full-page forms for longer messages. The headings *To, From,*

Date, and *Subject* are printed on the memos in a number of arrangements.

The first line of the body begins three or four lines below the headings. Short messages—not more than five lines—may be double spaced. Longer messages should be single spaced, with a double space between paragraphs.

The typist's reference initials are typed at the left margin a double space below the last line of the message. Enclosure notations, typed a double space below the reference initials, should be shown when something accompanies the memo.

Interoffice Memorandum

TO Thomas Crandall
FROM Susan Riley
DATE April 11, 19--
SUBJECT Report on Trip to Phoenix

The purpose of my trip to Phoenix on April 9-10 was: (1) to hold discussions with Mr. James Taylor, Phoenix branch office manager, regarding the new office procedures manual developed to modernize our procedures; (2) to meet with Mr. John Titus, exhibit chairperson of the National Invitational Skateboard Tournament, to discuss the exhibit we are planning; (3) to present the first quarter sales report to the regional sales representatives; (4) to hold informal discussions with Mr. Ronald Waverly of the Olympic Committee regarding the status of skateboarding as an Olympic sport; and (5) to discuss with Ms. Renee Switzer any ways we could be of assistance to the judges for the National Invitational Skateboard Tournament.

Mr. Taylor had thoroughly studied the new office procedures manual and was already implementing the new procedures.

Mr. Titus was very excited about the manner in which we plan to stage our exhibit and felt that the demonstrations would be extremely well attended. As a matter of fact, he has suggested that we use the adjacent hall as our exhibit area to provide for the anticipated crowds.

The regional representatives cheered the news of our increased sales for the first quarter and indicated that they would work even harder in the months ahead. Needless to say, the news of increased bonuses also helped to fire their enthusiasm.

Although the evening spent with Mr. Waverly was very pleasant, no additional information was gained regarding whether skateboarding would be accepted as an Olympic event in the near future. Mr. Waverly did agree that, because of the wide acceptance of the sport, strong consideration should be given.

Ms. Switzer requested that we again furnish a table of the degree of difficulty of events for the freestyle skating judges. I assured her that we would be able to provide this service.

In my opinion, the time spent on the trip was a good investment. I believe that it resulted in additional goodwill for the company that will eventually show up in increased sales.

xx

Figure 9-12   Full-page memo

Interoffice Memorandum

To: Kelly Ryan   **From:** Hans Anderson   **Date:** May 24, 19--

Subject: Fourth of July Spectacular

      Plans are just about complete for all the activities of our Fourth of
July Spectacular. The only difficulty we have had is in regard to the
air show--"The Flying Circus"--which we have contracted with for two
shows. The problem lies with obtaining approval from the New Orleans
Safety Commission based on interpretation of its regulations regarding
crowd safety. We hope to conclude our discussions and reach an agreement within the next couple of days.

      I will keep you posted as to future developments.

      xx

Figure 9-13   Half-page memo

COMPUTER DYNAMICS
Interoffice Memorandum

TO: Maria Valdez, C. W. Willard, Jan Reubew

FROM: Jon Richards

DATE: May 16, 19--

SUBJECT: Production Schedule

      Because of the Memorial Day holiday, it will be necessary to prepare

Figure 9-14   Multiple-address memo

INTEROFFICE MEMORANDUM

TO: Distribution List *

Distribution: Mark Everett
                Susan Riley
                Fred Symmes
                Frank Tomosh
                Lori Waltman
                Maureen Wilson

Figure 9-15   Distribution list memo

9.37 Interoffice memos are often sent to more than one person. When this occurs, the names of all the recipients should be shown on the *To* line.

Some firms prefer to indicate a "distribution list" for multiple address memos.

FILING CORRESPONDENCE

9.38 Filing is the process of arranging and storing materials in an orderly manner so they can be located quickly and easily. The most common filing systems used in business are *alphabetic, geographic, subject,* and *numeric,* although other systems and variations of the systems are also used.

The following rules are generally followed in alphabetic filing systems. The rules are adapted from those recommended by the Association of Records Managers and Administrators; other variations of the rules are sometimes followed.

Alphabetizing Names

9.39 To place names in correct filing order, compare them unit by unit and letter by letter in the following order: surname (last name), first name or initial, middle name or initial.

Johnson, Harold
Jones, Delaine Marie
Jones, Delaine Nancy

Nothing Before Something

9.40 File a surname by itself before the same surname with a first name or initial. File a surname with an initial only before the same surname with a full first name beginning with the same letter. In other words, "nothing comes before something."

Names	Alphabetical Order
Linda Mack	Mack
Mack	Mack, Linda
Linda T. Mack	Mack, Linda T.

Names with Prefixes and Hyphens

9.41 Prefixes in the names of individuals and companies (such as De Marco Fuel Company) are considered to be part of the surname.

Some common prefixes are *d'*, *Da*, *De*, *Del*, *Des*, *Di*, *Du*, *Fitz*, *La*, *Mac*, *Mc*, *O'*, *San*, *St.*, *Van*, and *Vander*. In filing, *St.* is filed as if it were spelled in full (Saint).

9.42   Hyphenated surnames (such as Ryan-Moore) are filed as only one unit.

Names	Alphabetical Order
Jill Santo-Rondo	St. Francis, James
James St. Francis	San August, Juan
Juan San August	Santo-Rondo, Jill

Unusual and Foreign Names

9.43   When it is difficult to determine which part of a name is the surname, consider the last name written to be the surname.

Names	Alphabetical Order
Hinson Henny	Henny, Hinson
Leu Viet Ho	Henry, Pasquel
Pasquel Henry	Ho, Leu Viet

Identical Names

9.44   When two or more personal or business names are identical, use the address to determine the correct filing order. Compare the parts of the address in the following order: (1) town or city name, (2) state name, (3) street name, and (4) house or building number in numeric order.

Names	Alphabetical Order
Mary Hart 116 Main Street Columbus, OH 43215	Hart, Mary, 287 Main Street, Columbus, GA 31003
Mary Hart 103 Main Street Columbus, OH 43215	Hart, Mary, 103 Main Street, Columbus, OH 43215
Mary Hart 287 Main Street Columbus, GA 31003	Hart, Mary, 116 Main Street, Columbus, OH 43215

Titles and Degrees

9.45   When identical names have seniority titles (such as Jr., Sr., II, III), use the seniority designations only to determine the order of filing. File Junior (Jr.) and Senior (Sr.) alphabetically; II and III, numerically.

.46 Do not consider professional titles (such as Dr. or Prof.), personal titles (such as Mr. or Miss), and academic degrees (such as Ph.D. or B.A.) in filing. Place them in parentheses after the name.

.47 When a religious, foreign, or royalty title is followed by a first name only, file the name as written.

Names	Alphabetical Order
Marina Martin, Ph.D.	Father Martin
Father Martin	Martin, Maria (Dr.)
Ralph W. Martin, Sr.	Martin, Marina (Ph.D.)
Ralph W. Martin, Jr.	Martin, Ralph W. (Jr.)
Dr. Maria Martin	Martin, Ralph W. (Sr.)

Names of Married Women

.48 File a married woman's legal name in the following order: (1) her husband's surname, (2) her first name or initial, and (3) her middle or maiden name. As with other titles, place *Mrs.* in parentheses after the name.

Names	Alphabetical Order
Mrs. John Page (Lois Smith)	Page, Lois Smith (Mrs.)
Mrs. Harry Payton (Lila Mae)	Parker, Lorraine Mae (Mrs.)
Mrs. Charles Parker (Lorraine Mae)	Payton, Lila Mae (Mrs.)

Company Names

.49 File a company name as it is written unless it includes the full name of an individual.

.50 If a company name includes the full name of an individual, file the name in the following order: (1) individual's surname, (2) individual's first name or initial, (3) individual's middle name or initial, and (4) the rest of the company name as written.

Names	Alphabetical Order
Abby T. Barneside Furniture	Acme Freight Company
Ron J. Adams Antiques	Adams, Ron J. Antiques
Acme Freight Company	Barneside, Abby T. Furniture

Articles, Conjunctions, and Prepositions

9.51 Do not consider articles and conjunctions when filing company names; place them in parentheses.

9.52 If a preposition is the first word of a company name, it is the first filing unit. Otherwise, do not consider it in filing and place it in parentheses.

Names	Alphabetical Order
The Onyx House	On Our Own Cafe
On Our Own Cafe	(The) Onyx House
Owens and Johns Market	Owens (and) Johns Market

Abbreviations and Single Letters

9.53 File abbreviations in a company name as if they were spelled in full.

9.54 If a company name is made up of single letters, each letter is a separate filing unit.

Names	Alphabetical Order
WC Restaurant	WC Restaurant
Geo. Wise Jewelry	Wilson Company
Wilson Co.	Wise, George Jewelry

Hyphenated Company Names

9.55 Company names that include hyphenated last names (such as Ryan-Jones Company), coined words (such as Rite-Lite Bulb Company), and other hyphenated forms (such as Mid-Continent Oil Co.) are filed as if the hyphenated parts were one unit.

Names	Alphabetical Order
Cutler-Martin Book Store	C-Out Glass Company
Cow-Town Stockyards	Cow-Town Stockyards
C-Out Glass Co.	Cutler-Martin Book Store

Compass Points in Company Names

9.56 Each compass point in a company name is a separate filing unit. Treat compass points as separate words even if they are written together (North = 1 unit; Northeast = 2 units, *North* and *east*).

Names	Alphabetical Order
Northern Hats, Inc.	Northeast Builders

North West Truckers   North West Truckers
Northeast Builders   Northern Hats, Incorporated

Numbers in Company Names

9.57 Numerals in company names (such as 57 Club) are not spelled out
and are filed in strict numeric order in front of everything else in the
alphabetic file. File company names with spelled-out numbers alphabetically.

Names	Alphabetical Order
Third Floor Salon	23 Skidoo Dance Studio
Ten Sisters Cafe	Ten Sisters Cafe
23 Skidoo Dance Studio	Third Floor Salon

Schools and Colleges

9.58 File the names of elementary, middle, and high schools as written
unless they contain full personal names. File the names of colleges
and universities by the most important part of their names.

Names	Alphabetical Order
Austin College	Akron, University (of)
Gene Austin High School	Austin College
University of Akron	Austin, Gene High School

Churches and Organizations

9.59 File names of churches, synagogues, clubs, and organizations as written.

Names	Alphabetical Order
Friends & Neighbors Club	First Methodist Church
Fraternal Order of Seagulls	Fraternal Order (of) Seagulls
First Methodist Church	Friends (&) Neighbors Club

Magazines and Newspapers

9.60 File the names of magazines and newspapers as written. If the names
are identical, use the city (and state if necessary) as the last filing unit.

Names	Alphabetical Order
The Daily Herald (Moline)	(The) Daily Herald, Minneapolis
Modern Home Magazine	(The) Daily Herald, Moline
The Daily Herald (Minneapolis)	Modern Home Magazine

Hotels and Motels

9.61 Reverse names beginning with "Hotel" and "Motel" so that the most important part of the name is the first unit. File other hotel and motel names as written.

Names	Alphabetical Order
Royal Inn	Redwood Hotel
Hotel Redwood	Royal Inn
Motel Royale	Royale Motel

Government Agencies

9.62 When filing the names of federal government agencies, the words "United States Government" are the first three filing units, followed by (1) name of the department, (2) name of the bureau, (3) name of the division or subdivision, and (4) title of the official.

9.63 When filing the names of state, county, or city agencies, the particular state, county, or city name is the first filing unit, followed by the word "State," "County," or "City." The department, bureau, and/or title of the official are the next filing units.

Place terms such as "department," "department of," and "division" in parentheses and do not consider them in filing.

Names	Alphabetical Order
U.S. Department of Commerce	Denver, City, Police (Dept.)
Hinds County Welfare Dept.	Hinds, County, Welfare (Dept.)
Denver Police Department	United States Government, Commerce (Dept. of)

Filing Systems

9.64 Among the most frequently used filing systems are the following:

ALPHABETIC: Correspondence is filed alphabetically using standard filing rules.

GEOGRAPHIC: Correspondence is filed according to location—regions, states, cities, and so on.

SUBJECT: Correspondence is filed according to major categories of subject matter.

NUMERIC: Correspondence is filed by number—ZIP Code, policy number, account number, telephone number, or by a number assigned to each company or person.

All other filing systems are generally variations of one of the four basic types.

Self-Check Exercise

SECTION I

From the list at the right, select the term that matches the description at the left. Write the letter of your selection in the space provided.

_____ 1. May also include company insignia, slogan, and telephone number

_____ 2. Letter in which all lines begin at left margin except date and closing lines

_____ 3. Letter in which all lines begin at left margin

_____ 4. May be typed in all capital letters a double space below the complimentary close

_____ 5. Used for one- and two-page letters and letters with enclosures

_____ 6. Used for sending statements to customers

_____ 7. Used for one-page letters and small letterheads

_____ 8. Does not contain salutation or complimentary close

_____ 9. Number of *creases* in a letter inserted in a No. $6\frac{3}{4}$ envelope

_____ 10. Used for messages within a firm

_____ 11. Indicates who typed the letter

_____ 12. Used to indicate that copies are sent without knowledge of addressee

_____ 13. Number of *creases* in a letter inserted in a No. 10 envelope

A. AMS Simplified style

B. Blind copy notation

C. Block style

D. Company name

E. Interoffice memorandum

F. Letterhead

G. Modified block style

H. No. $6\frac{3}{4}$ envelope

I. No. 10 envelope

J. Reference initials

K. Three

L. Two

M. Window envelope

SECTION II

Arrange the following list of letter parts in the order in which they would appear in a business letter. Write the numbers 1–18 in the blanks provided.

_____ Attention line   _____ Postscript

_____ Body   _____ Printed letterhead

_____ Company name   _____ Reference initials

_____ Complimentary close   _____ Salutation

_____ Copy notation   _____ Separate cover notation

_____ Date   _____ Signature

_____ Enclosure notation   _____ Subject line

_____ Inside address   _____ Title

_____ Mailing notation   _____ Typed name

SECTION III

Place the names in Column A in correct alphabetical order in Column B by listing the numbers preceding the names.

Column A

1. Robt. W. Davis, Jr.
2. Davis
3. Delaine D'Antonio
4. Denson Davis
5. Davidson Hardware
   100 Main Street
   Jackson, MS
6. Mrs. D. H. Dalton (Lucy)
7. Davidson Hardware
   101 Main Street
   Jackson, TN
8. D-Lite Diner
9. 16 Trees Cafe
10. Dallas Police Department

Column B

_____

_____

_____

_____

_____

_____

_____

_____

_____

_____

Check your answers in the back of the book.

10 Business Reports

REPORTS of various types are commonly used to communicate with persons within and outside the company to present information and to help make effective decisions. They may be short or long, informal or formal. While procedures vary from office to office, there are some generally established rules for preparing reports that should be followed.

OUTLINE

10.1 The outline (see Figure 10-1) is the skeletal organization for the report and is generally prepared first. It helps the writer decide on the organization and content. It indicates the major divisions, the secondary topics, and the supporting data.

10.2 Outlines use Roman numerals to identify the major divisions, capital letters to identify secondary topics, and Arabic numerals to identify major points. If still other divisions are needed, lowercase letters and Arabic numerals in parentheses can be used. Since an outline represents the divisions of material, there must be at least two entries for each level of heading. For example, if there is a I, there must be a II; if there is an A, there must be a B; if there is a 1, there must be a 2. An example of an outline showing the appropriate divisions and spacing follows.

10

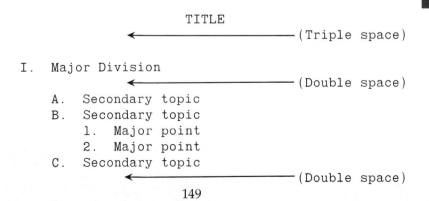

```
                        TITLE
              ←————————————————(Triple space)

     I.   Major Division
                  ←————————————————(Double space)
          A.   Secondary topic
          B.   Secondary topic
               1.   Major point
               2.   Major point
          C.   Secondary topic
                  ←————————————————(Double space)
```

```
 II.  Major Division
                    ←————————————————— (Double space)
      A.  Secondary topic
          1.  Major point
          2.  Major point
              a.  Minor point
              b.  Minor point
                  (1)  Supporting data
                  (2)  Supporting data
      B.  Secondary topic
                    ←————————————————— (Double space)
III.  Major Division
```

Align the periods following the various levels of headings. Two spaces follow the periods at each division level.

10.3 Outlines may be written in topic form or sentence form. The *topic form* lists the divisions of the outline in small word groups, phrases, or clauses. The *sentence form* uses complete sentences for the major divisions.

Related divisions of the outline should be parallel in structure. That is, if one division begins with a verb, all related divisions should begin with verbs; if one division begins with a noun, all related divisions should begin with nouns.

BUSINESS REPORTS

10.4 Brief, informal reports may be in the form of a business letter or interoffice memorandum. (See Figures 10-2 and 10-3.)

10.5 Formal reports may be rather lengthy and detailed and contain most or all of the following parts.

```
 1. Cover            ⎫
 2. Title page       ⎪
 3. Letter of transmittal ⎪
 4. Preface          ⎬  Introductory
 5. Table of contents ⎪     Pages
 6. List of tables and charts ⎪
 7. Summary          ⎭
 8. Introduction     ⎫  Body of the
 9. Text of the report ⎬    Report
10. Conclusions      ⎭
11. Appendix         ⎫  Supplementary
12. Bibliography     ⎬     Pages
13. Index            ⎭
```

Cover

10.6 Type the cover for the report on paper of the same quality as that used for the report itself. It contains only the title of the report, typed in all capital letters, centered vertically and horizontally. (See Figure 10-4.)

Title Page

10.7 The title page contains the title of the report, the writer's name and title, and the date. Space the items on the title page attractively, with each line centered horizontally. (See Figure 10-5.)

Letter of Transmittal

10.8 The letter of transmittal, which may take the place of a preface, is addressed to the person requesting or authorizing the report. It usually contains information regarding the purpose of the report, the scope of the report, methods of gathering information, findings, and conclusions. Type the letter on letterhead stationery, using the customary letter style.

If a preface is also prepared for the report, the letter of transmittal serves only as a cover letter to indicate what is enclosed.

Preface

10.9 The preface may be used in place of an introduction to the report. It provides information regarding the purpose, scope, general findings, and conclusions.

Table of Contents

10.10 The table of contents lists the page numbers of the parts of the report and the major headings in the body of the report (as shown on the outline). A table of contents need not be prepared unless the report is lengthy or unless there are many divisions within the report. It is not prepared until the rest of the report is typed so that the page numbers will be accurate. (See Figure 10-6.)

The table of contents should be attractively placed on the page. Leaders, made by alternately striking the period and the space bar, may or may not be used.

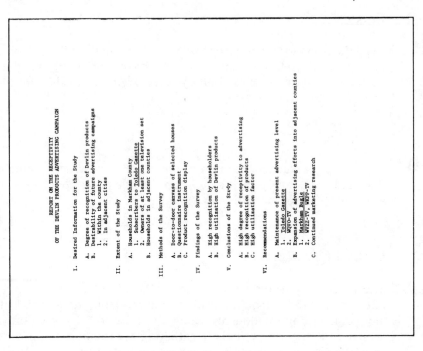

Figure 10-1   Report outline

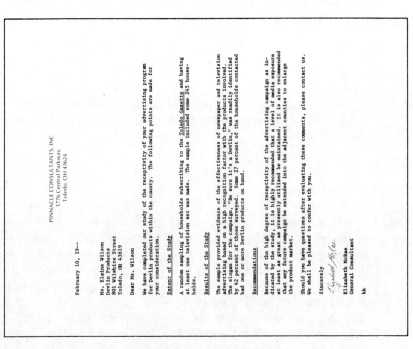

Figure 10-2   Business letter report

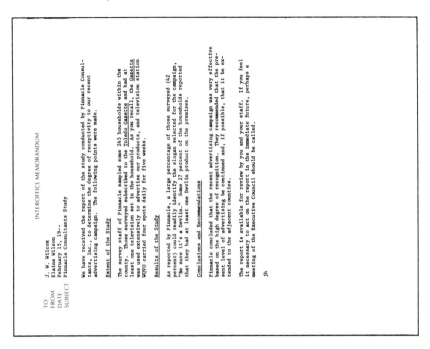

INTEROFFICE MEMORANDUM

TO: J. W. Wilcox
FROM: Elaine Wilson
DATE: February 15, 19--
SUBJECT: Pinnacle Consultants Study

We have received the report of the study conducted by Pinnacle Consultants, Inc., to determine the degree of receptivity to our recent advertising campaign. The following points were made.

Extent of the Study

The survey staff of Pinnacle sampled some 245 households within the county. Those surveyed subscribed to the Toledo Gazette and had at least one television set in the household. As you recall, the Gazette was used extensively to advertise our products, and television station WQVO carried four spots daily for five weeks.

Results of the Study

As reported by Pinnacle, a large percentage of those surveyed (42 percent) could readily identify the slogan selected for the campaign, "Be sure it's a Devlin." Some 27 percent of the households reported that they had at least one Devlin product on the premises.

Conclusions and Recommendations

Pinnacle concluded that the recent advertising campaign was very effective based on the high degree of recognition. They recommended that the present level of advertising be continued and, if possible, that it be extended to the adjacent counties.

The report is available for review by you and your staff. If you feel it necessary to act on the report in the immediate future, perhaps a meeting of the Executive Council should be called.

jh

Figure 10-3   Interoffice memorandum report

REPORT ON THE RECEPTIVITY
OF THE DEVLIN PRODUCTS ADVERTISING CAMPAIGN

Figure 10-4   Report cover

Figure 10-5   Report title page

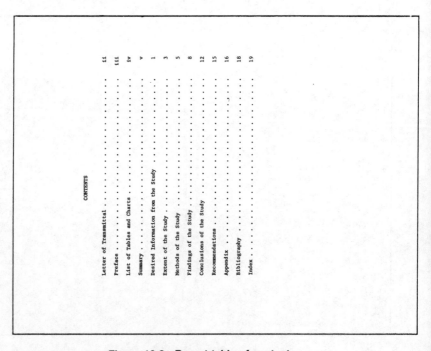

Figure 10-6   Report table of contents

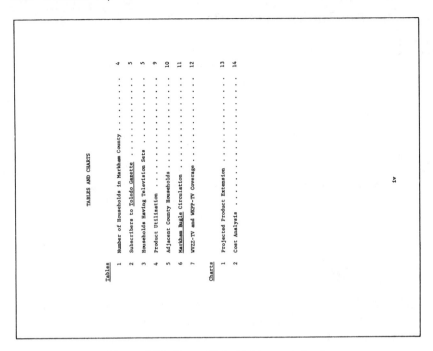

TABLES AND CHARTS

Tables

1 Number of Households in Markham County 4

2 Subscribers to Toledo Gazette 5

3 Households Having Television Sets 5

4 Product Utilization 9

5 Adjacent County Households 10

6 Markham Bugle Circulation 11

7 WVZZ-TV and WKFP-TV Coverage 12

Charts

1 Projected Product Extension 13

2 Cost Analysis 14

iv

Figure 10-7   Report list of tables and charts

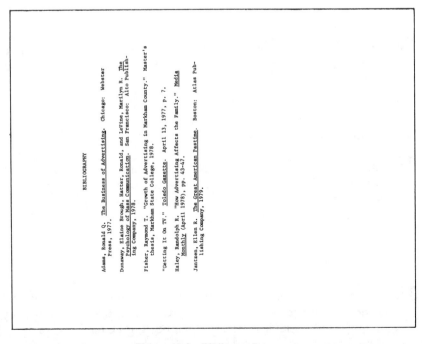

BIBLIOGRAPHY

Adams, Ronald Q. The Business of Advertising. Chicago: Webster Press, 1977.

Dunaway, Elaine Brough, Hatter, Ronald, and LeVine, Marilyn R. The Psychology of Mass Communication. San Francisco: Alto Publishing Company, 1978.

Fisher, Raymond T. "Growth of Advertising in Markham County." Master's thesis, Markham State College, 1978.

"Getting It On TV." Toledo Gazette, April 13, 1977, p. 7.

Haley, Randolph R. "How Advertising Affects the Family." Media Monthly (April 1978), pp. 43-47.

Jantzen, Ellen R. The Great American Pastime. Boston: Atlas Publishing Company, 1979.

Figure 10-8   Bibliography

List of Tables and Charts

10.11 If the report includes many tables and charts, prepare a separate page listing the items, using the same format as the table of contents. (See Figure 10-7.)

Summary

10.12 The summary of the report, prepared after the text has been written, presents major points, significant findings, conclusions, and recommendations. It provides the reader with a quick overview of the report.

Introduction

10.13 The introduction to the report provides the reader with the reasons and purposes of the report, sources of information, how the information was gathered, scope of the report, and how the information is to be presented.

Text of the Report

10.14 The text of the report is the main body of the report including the discussion, proposals, findings, etc. It should follow the divisions reflected in the report outline.

Conclusions

10.15 The writer's conclusions, based on the information provided in the report itself, may be presented in a list or in strict narrative form. Recommendations or suggested actions may also be a part of this section.

Appendix

10.16 An appendix presents additional information or illustrations that expand or interpret the information provided in the body of the report. It may contain tables, surveys, supporting statements, or technical data.

Bibliography

10.17   The bibliography is a complete listing of all sources referred to or used by the writer in preparing the report. It may include books, periodicals, government publications, and articles. References in the bibliography should be listed in alphabetical order by author or, if the authors' names are not given, by titles or editors. (See Figure 10-8.)

Index

10.18   Prepare an index if the report is especially lengthy and detailed. It is compiled after the body of the report has been completed and lists all topics, subtopics, tables, and charts in the report and the pages on which they are found. An index assists the reader in locating specific information in the body of the report.

TYPING THE REPORT

Reports may be unbound; that is, in loose sheets placed in a folder. They may also be bound (stapled or otherwise secured) at the top or at the left. The following margins are generally followed for each of these situations.

10.19   **Unbound**
   1. A top margin of 2 inches on the first page, 1 inch on succeeding pages.
   2. Left, right, and bottom margins of 1 inch.

10.20   **Bound at the top**
   1. A top margin of 2½ inches on the first page, 1½ inches on succeeding pages.
   2. Left, right, and bottom margins of 1 inch.

10.21   **Bound at the left**
   1. A top margin of 2 inches on the first page, 1 inch on succeeding pages.
   2. A left margin of 1½ inches.
   3. Bottom and right margins of 1 inch.

Paging the Report

10.22   Introductory pages are generally numbered with small Roman numerals. Although it is not numbered, the title page is considered to be "i." Beginning with "ii" (usually the letter of transmittal), the page numbers are typed at the center, $\frac{1}{2}$ inch from the bottom of the page.

10.23 Number all pages within the body of the report with Arabic numerals, beginning with page 1 and running consecutively throughout the rest of the report. Some typists prefer to omit the page number on the first page. Typed page numbers then begin with page 2.

Type the page number for the first page at the center, $\frac{1}{2}$ inch from the bottom of the page. Unless the report is bound at the top, type other page numbers even with the right margin $\frac{1}{2}$ inch from the top of the page. Type all page numbers for top-bound reports at the center, $\frac{1}{2}$ inch from the bottom of the page.

Spacing

10.24 Center the *title* of the report, typed in all capital letters, 2 inches from the top of the first page. If the report is to be bound at the left, center the title over the report, not the center of the paper.

If the title is followed by a centered heading, double space after the title and triple space after the centered heading. If the title is followed by the text of the report, triple space.

10.25 The *body* of the report is always double spaced, with five-space paragraph indentions. If quotations of four or more typed lines appear, single space them and indent five spaces from both the left and right margins. Quotations of less than four typed lines may be double spaced and run into the text. If numbered lists of items appear, type them single spaced.

10.26 *Centered headings* relate to the major divisions of an outline as indicated by the Roman numerals. Triple space before these headings and double space after them. They are usually typed in all capital letters, but they may be typed in capitals and lowercase and underlined.

10.27 *Secondary headings* used within the body of the report relate to the divisions of the outline represented by capital letters. Leave a triple space before them and a double space after. Type these headings in capitals and lowercase letters, underlined, at the left margin. Capitalize only the first and important words.

10.28 *Paragraph headings* relate to the division of the outline represented by Arabic numerals. They begin at the paragraph indention point and "run into" the paragraph itself. Double space only above these headings. Capitalize only the first word and underline the entire heading. The heading is usually followed by a period.

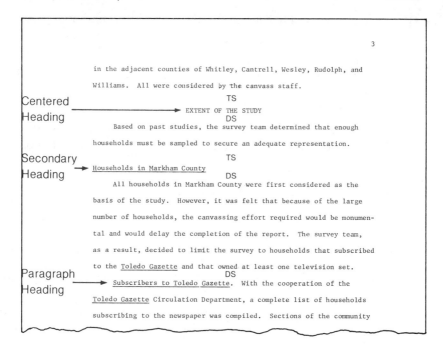

Figure 10-9   Headings for a report

FOOTNOTES

10.29   Footnotes give credit for quoted material and provide additional information or details. The footnote is indicated at the point of reference by a superior figure. The footnote is generally placed at the bottom of the page on which the reference occurs. Footnotes are usually numbered consecutively throughout the report. (See Figure 10-10.)

at least four hours daily.[1]

    In all cases, the household had access to at least one television set. In most cases, the members of the survey team determined that the

---

[1]Ellen R. Jantzen, *The Great American Pastime* (Boston: Atlas Publishing Company, 1979), p. 108.

Figure 10-10   Footnote

10.30 Footnotes generally contain the following information:

1. Author's name (in reading order)
2. Title of author's work
3. Publication information: city of publication, name of publisher, publication date
4. Volume and page references, if available

   If the item referred to is from a periodical, enclose the title of the article in quotation marks while underlining the name of the periodical.

10.31 Follow these guidelines in typing footnotes:

1. Type a $1\frac{1}{2}$-inch separating line a single space below the last line of the text. Double space after the line.
2. Indent the first line of each footnote, the same number of spaces as the paragraph indentions.
3. Be sure to use the same superior number for the footnote as for the reference in the text.
4. Single space each footnote with a double space between footnotes.
5. Leave a 1-inch bottom margin below the last line of the footnote.

10.32 Footnotes may also be typed together in a list on a separate page at the end of the report. If this practice is followed, center the word "Notes," typed in all capital letters, 2 inches from the top of the page. Then triple space and type the notes in numerical order, single spaced, with a double space between the notes.

BIBLIOGRAPHY

10.33 A bibliography is a complete list of all the sources referred to or used by the writer in compiling the report. The bibliography is generally typed on a separate page and placed at the end of the report. (See Figure 10-8.)

10.34 Type the word "Bibliography" in all capital letters, centered 2 inches from the top of the page. The first entry begins a triple space below this heading. The bibliography is single spaced with a double space between entries. The first line of each entry in the bibliography begins at the left margin, with second and succeeding lines in each entry indented.

10.35 The entries in the bibliography are arranged in alphabetical order by author, or by title if there is no author. Each entry should contain the following information:

1. *Author's name, last name first.* If there is more than one author, transpose all names.
2. *Title of the source.* Underline the title of a book or periodical; enclose the title of a magazine article in quotation marks.
3. *Publication information.* For a book, list the city of publication, name of the publisher, and date of publication. For an article, list the name of the publication, the volume number, the date of publication, and the page numbers.

Note that in a bibliography entry, a *period* is used to separate the parts.

PREPARING TABLES

Tabular material should be prepared so that it has a pleasant appearance and is easy to read and interpret. Tables may utilize major and secondary headings, as well as column headings.

10.36 To determine the vertical placement of the material:

1. Count the number of typed and blank lines in the material.
2. Subtract the number found in step 1 from 66, if using a full sheet of paper, or from 33, if using a half sheet of paper.
3. Divide this remainder by 2. The answer is the number of blank lines to be left at the top and bottom of the page.
4. If you want the material to have more blank space at the bottom than at the top (often referred to as "reading position"), subtract 3 lines from the answer you arrived at in step 3.

There are two methods used to determine horizontal placement of tabulated material.

Mathematical Method

10.37 To determine horizontal placement of the material using the mathematical method, follow these steps:

1. Clear all tab stops and move the left and right margins to their farthest points left and right.
2. Count the number of letters, punctuation marks, and spaces in the longest item or heading in each column. Determine the total for all columns.

3. Decide on the number of spaces you wish to leave between the columns, usually between four and ten spaces. Add the spaces to be left between columns to the figure you arrived at in step 2 (the total spaces required for the items in all the columns).
4. Subtract the answer in step 3 from 102 for elite typewriters or 85 for pica typewriters. Divide by 2 to find the left margin.
5. To the left margin, add the number of spaces in the longest item in column 1 plus the number of spaces to be left between columns 1 and 2. Set your first tab stop; this is the beginning point of column 2.
6. To the first tab stop, add the number of spaces in the longest item in column 2 plus the number of spaces to be left between columns 2 and 3. Set the tab stop; this is the beginning of column 3. Continue in this way until all tab stops are set.

Mathematical Method of Horizontal Placement

Step 1:   Clear tabs and margins.

Step 2:
    11   (first column—Centerville)
    10   (second column—Population)
  +11   (third column—Subscribers)
    32

Step 3:
    32   (total from step 2)
     8   (spaces between columns 1 and 2)
  + 8   (spaces between columns 2 and 3)
    48

Step 4:

ELITE
  102 (elite spaces)
 − 48 (total from step 3)
2) 54
   27 (left margin)

PICA
  85 (pica spaces)
−48
2) 37
 18 (left margin)

Step 5:
ELITE
  27 (left margin)
  11 (longest item, column 1)
+ 8 (spaces between columns)
 46 first tab

PICA
 18 (left margin)
 11
+ 8
 37 first tab

Step 6:
  46 (first tab)
  10 (longest item, column 2)
+ 8 (spaces between columns)
 64 second tab

 37 (first tab)
 10
+ 8
 55 second tab

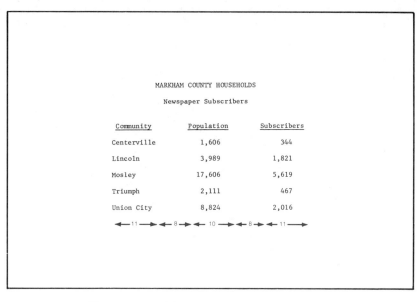

MARKHAM COUNTY HOUSEHOLDS

Newspaper Subscribers

Community	Population	Subscribers
Centerville	1,606	344
Lincoln	3,989	1,821
Mosley	17,606	5,619
Triumph	2,111	467
Union City	8,824	2,016

Figure 10-11   Using the mathematical method

Backspace Method

10.38 To determine horizontal placement of the material using the backspace method, follow these steps:

1. Clear all tab stops and move the left and right margins to their farthest points left and right.
2. Decide on the number of spaces you wish to leave between columns, usually between four and ten spaces.
3. Beginning at the center of the page, backspace once for every two letters, punctuation marks, and spaces in the longest item or heading in each column. Backspace once for every two spaces to be left between columns. Set the left margin at this point. This is the beginning point for column 1.
4. From the left margin, space once for each letter, punctuation mark, and space in the longest item in column 1; space once for every space to be left between column 1 and column 2. Set the first tab at this point; this is the beginning point for column 2.
5. From the first tab stop, space once for every letter, punctuation mark, and space in the longest item in column 2; space once for every space to be left between column 2 and column 3. Set the second tab at this point; this is the beginning point for column 3. Continue in this way until all tab stops are set.

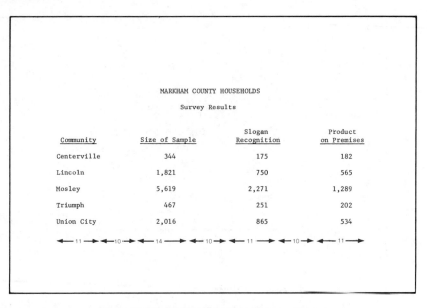

MARKHAM COUNTY HOUSEHOLDS

Survey Results

Community	Size of Sample	Slogan Recognition	Product on Premises
Centerville	344	175	182
Lincoln	1,821	750	565
Mosley	5,619	2,271	1,289
Triumph	467	251	202
Union City	2,016	865	534

Figure 10-12   Using the backspace method

Headings for Tables

10.39 The title of the table is typed in all capital letters and centered horizontally. Subheadings are generally centered, typed a double space below the title in capitals and lowercase letters. Triple space after subheadings or the main heading if subheadings are not used. Column headings are centered over the columns. Column headings are usually typed in capitals and lowercase letters and underlined. Column headings may be broken into more than one line if necessary.

The body of the table may be single or double spaced, depending on the length of the table and the degree of readability desired.

Self-Check Exercise

SECTION I

Write the name of the term defined by the statement in the blank to the left.

_____ 1. The skeletal organization for a manuscript or report

_____ 2. Lists the beginning page numbers for the major divisions of the report

_____ 3. Lists the title of the report, the writer's name and title, and the date

_____ 4. Lists all topics, subtopics, tables, and charts in the report and the pages on which they are found; assists the reader in finding specific information in the body of the report

_____ 5. Gives credit for quoted material and provides additional information

_____ 6. Lists all the sources referred to or used by the writer

_____ 7. Takes the place of a preface to the report or serves as a cover letter

_____ 8. Helps expand or interpret the information provided in the body of the report; may contain tables, surveys, or supporting statements

_____ 9. Provides the reader with the reasons and purposes of the report and how the information will be presented

_____ 10. Presents the discussion, proposals, findings; follows the divisions reflected in the report outline

SECTION II

Select the correct word from those in parentheses below by circling the correct word.

1. (Roman, Arabic) numerals are used to identify the major divisions in an outline.
2. (Two, Three) spaces follow periods in an outline.
3. The body of a report is (single, double) spaced.
4. In the body of a report, quotations of more than four typed lines are (single, double) spaced.
5. In an unbound report, the left, right, and bottom margins are (1, $1\frac{1}{2}$) inch(es).
6. The left margin of a report bound at the left is (1, $1\frac{1}{2}$) inch(es).
7. Footnotes are (single, double) spaced.
8. Leave a (double, triple) space above centered headings.
9. Introductory pages are usually numbered in small (Arabic, Roman) numerals.
10. The (index, summary) provides the reader with a quick overview of the report.

Check your answers in the back of the book.

11 Using Communications Systems

BUSINESSES use a variety of methods to communicate with customers, employees, the general public, and other businesses. The two most widely used methods are the postal system and the telephone. Telegrams and mailgrams are also used.

A basic understanding of these various methods, rates and restrictions, special services available, and speed will be of value to all office personnel.

POSTAL SERVICES

11.1 Since postal services are used in almost every business office, it is imperative that office personnel be familiar with the restrictions, rates, classes, and special services. Certain materials cannot be mailed—explosives, intoxicating beverages, radioactive materials, and firearms. Rates seem to change every year. Weight and size requirements for the various classes of mail change from time to time. Special services have increased to take care of the needs of the public.

For the most up-to-date information, it is best to refer to a current copy of the *Postal Service Manual*, which can be obtained by writing to the Superintendent of Documents, U.S. Government Printing Office, Washington, DC 20402. The Post Office also issues bulletins that update and summarize postal information.

First Class

11.2 First-class mail receives high-priority handling by the Postal Service. That is, it is generally handled before other classes of mail. First-class mail may be sent anywhere in the United States, its territories, to the armed forces, and to Canada and Mexico.

11.3 First-class mail consists of the following items, which meet other general postal requirements:

1. *All matter sealed against postal inspection.*
2. *Bills and statements of account.*
3. *Letters.* The handling of personal and business letters is a major part of the responsibility of the Postal Service. First-class mail is

most frequently used for normal business communications.

4. *Postal cards.* A postal card is a card supplied by the Postal Service with a postage stamp printed or impressed on it.
5. *Post cards.* These are privately printed mailing cards, such as picture post cards, used for sending messages.

Also included is any other matter totally or partly in writing or typewriting, except certain items such as newspapers, magazines, books, and catalogues that are considered to be second- or third-class mail. The cost of mailing first-class materials is based on each ounce or fraction of an ounce.

11.4 To process first-class mail at a faster rate, the Postal Service has implemented many improvements. Mail sorting is more rapid through the use of optical character readers as well as mechanical sorters. Because of the mechanized mail handling, certain size and shape limitations have been imposed.

11.5 The following standards presently apply to size and shape of first-class envelopes and cards.

1. Envelopes must be at least $3\frac{1}{2}$ inches by 5 inches.
2. Envelopes more than $6\frac{1}{8}$ inches by $11\frac{1}{2}$ inches are considered nonstandard. A surcharge is usually added to the cost of regular postage for the handling of any items that exceed these dimensions.
3. Envelopes and cards must have rectangular shapes.
4. Very thin cards, those having a thickness of less than 0.006 of an inch, are not mailable.

Addresses on envelopes must, of course, be legible, accurate, and complete if the automated equipment is to be utilized effectively. See Section 9.32 for information on the proper addressing of envelopes.

Second Class

11.6 Second-class mail includes newspapers, magazines, and other periodicals published at least four times a year. Rates for second-class mail are determined by the weight of the item and the distance it must be mailed. There is no weight limit for second-class mail. Special bulk rates for large quantities of second-class materials are available by applying for a permit from the postmaster.

Third Class

11.7 Third-class mail consists of items weighing less than 16 ounces and not classified as first- or second-class mail. Third-class mail includes catalogues, newsletters, circulars, booklets, merchandise, seeds, and other items that guarantee payment of postage due, such as hotel and motel keys.

Rates for third-class mail are determined by the weight and mailing distance. Nonprofit organizations (religious, charitable, and benevolent societies, for example) may obtain special rates. Special bulk-mailing rates may be obtained by securing a permit from the postmaster.

Fourth Class

11.8 Fourth-class mail, often referred to as *parcel post,* includes merchandise, printed matter, mailable live animals, and other matter not included in the other classes of mail. Fourth-class mail must weigh at least 1 pound but not more than 70 pounds. It also must be no more than 100 inches in combined length and girth.

A special fourth-class rate is available for films, sheet music, recordings, books, catalogues, and certain library items weighing 1 pound or more.

A number of special services are available from the Postal Service at an additional charge.

Business Reply Mail

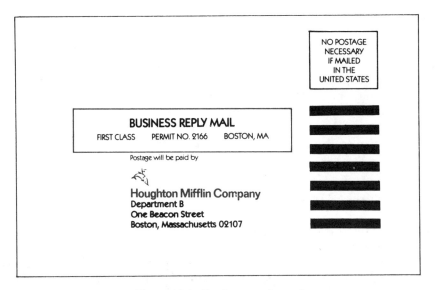

Figure 11-1   Business reply card

11.9 With a special permit, senders may mail cards, envelopes, and cartons to prospective customers from whom they need responses. The prospective customer does not pay the return postage for the response. Instead, the sender of business reply mail pays the first-class rate, plus an additional fee, when each piece is returned by the Postal Service.

Certified Mail

11.10 Any first-class matter that has no value in itself (such as a contract) can utilize this service. With this service the sender receives a receipt certifying that the item was mailed and delivered to the addressee. The addressee must sign for delivery.

Certified mail is handled like ordinary mail; there is no insurance coverage. The charge for certified mail is in addition to the regular postage. For an additional fee, restricted delivery and/or return receipt can be obtained.

Certificate of Mailing

11.11 When the sender wishes to have proof that an item was actually mailed, the sender's post office can issue a certificate of mailing. This certificate becomes proof of the mailing should it be needed in the future. A certificate of mailing may be used for all classes of mail except second class.

COD (Collect on Delivery)

11.12 By using COD (Collect on Delivery) service, an addressee may pay for an article, plus the cost of the postage, when it is delivered. The sender then receives the amount collected in the form of a postal money order. The sender, in turn, pays a fee for this service, which includes a charge for insurance.

First-, third-, and fourth-class materials may be sent as COD mail; however, the maximum amount collected from the addressee cannot exceed $300.

Express Mail

11.13 Express mail service provides guaranteed next-day delivery between most major metropolitan areas in the country for any letter or package weighing up to 70 pounds. Letters or packages taken to the express mail window of the post office by 5 P.M. are delivered to the addressee by 3 P.M. the following day.

Rates for this service are determined by the weight of the item and the distance it must travel.

Insured Mail

11.14 Third- and fourth-class mail can be insured against loss or damage for an additional fee. Liability for insured mail is limited to $200. Certain items, including very fragile articles and unauthorized material addressed to prospective purchasers, cannot be insured.

Postal Money Order

11.15 Postal money orders are a safe means of sending money through the mail. They may be purchased from any post office in amounts up to $100. Fees for money orders vary, depending on the amount of the money order. They must, however, be paid for in United States currency. They can be redeemed at any post office.

Registered Mail

11.16 Registered mail service provides added protection for valuable and important mail. It also provides evidence of mailing and delivery, as well as insurance (up to a maximum of $10,000) against loss or damage. The sender must declare the full value of the registered mail.

For an additional fee the sender can request a return receipt, which verifies delivery. Restricted delivery, which ensures delivery to the addressee only, can also be obtained for an additional fee.

Special Delivery

11.17 Within prescribed limitations, a special delivery item will be delivered immediately once it reaches its destination. This service does not affect the transportation time of the item between post offices but it will get preferential handling once it arrives at its destination.

All classes of mail can be sent special delivery for an additional charge. The weight and class of mail determine this charge.

Type or write the words "Special Delivery" immediately below the position for postage on items to be sent using this service.

Special Handling

11.18 Special handling is available for third- and fourth-class mail only. It provides preferential handling between post offices and delivery at the destination. It does not, however, provide for special delivery; rather a special handling item is transported and delivered before other third- and fourth-class items not having this service.

Type or write the words "Special Handling" immediately below the position for postage on items to be sent using this service.

International Mail

11.19 International mail may include letters, printed matter, and packages sent to any foreign country. It does not include mail sent to foreign countries through the U.S. military post offices.

11.20 *Aerogrammes* are a convenient way of sending brief messages at lower rates. They are printed on lightweight, prestamped paper that folds into an envelope. They can be purchased at any post office.

Rates for international mail depend on the weight, type of service, and travel distance. Contact the post office regarding rates, regulations, and restrictions.

National ZIP Code Directory

11.21 This publication is a national directory of all ZIP Codes and contains information on how to use ZIP Codes in addresses.

The ZIP (Zone Improvement Plan) Code, devised by the Postal Service, helps to speed delivery of the mail by assigning numbers to geographical locations.

Postal Service Manual

11.22 The U.S. Postal Service publishes the *Postal Service Manual*, which contains complete information about services, classes of mail, and rates. The *Manual*, available through the U.S. Government Printing Office, is updated by periodic supplements.

Postage Meters

11.23 A postage meter is a machine that can print the correct postage on envelopes or on a special tape for packages. Offices use postage meters to control and record the amount of postage used and, at the same time, eliminate the need for stamps of varying amounts. Metered mail, because it does not have to be canceled as does stamped mail, can be processed more quickly by the post office.

The meter must be taken to a post office where the postage is paid for in advance. A special meter is inserted that automatically subtracts the amount of postage used. In this way the user always knows the amount remaining.

TELEGRAMS AND MAILGRAMS

11.24 When it is necessary to send a brief, urgent message or when a written record of that message is important, a mailgram or telegram may be sent. Telegrams and mailgrams are frequently used to attract the attention of a busy person.

   The mailgram utilizes the services of Western Union and the U.S. Postal Service; the telegram is sent and received through the facilities of Western Union.

Mailgrams

11.25 Messages for mailgrams may be given to Western Union for transmission by telephone, Telex, TWX, computer, or other communicating devices such as communicating typewriters, data terminals, or facsimile devices. Messages given to Western Union by 5 P.M. will be delivered the next business day.

   Mailgrams assure speedy delivery at low cost. They give the appearance of an urgent message because they are printed to look like telegrams. Mailgrams can be charged to your telephone bill.

11.26 The base cost of a 100-word, telephone-originated message is about $3. The word count includes all elements—name, address, salutation, text, closing, and sender's name. All letters and most symbols can be used in the message.

11.27 No special form is needed in preparing the message. If the message is telephoned to Western Union for transmission, a typed copy of the message should be prepared for the file. For a nominal charge you may request a copy of the mailgram.

11.28 Mailgrams are sent electronically to the post office nearest the addressee, where they are typed on high-speed typewriters on special mailgram forms. After insertion in a special envelope, they are delivered by the regular mail carriers.

Telegrams

11.29 Telegrams are a rapid method of transmitting messages using the communication facilities of Western Union. Telegrams can be sent 24 hours a day, including Sundays and holidays. Telegrams can be phoned in to the Western Union office or they can be placed over the counter or through other communications devices. In most instances they can be delivered within two hours by telephone and within five hours by messenger service.

11.30 Overnight telegrams, which offer message delivery by 2 P.M. the following day, can be sent at a substantially lower cost than regular telegrams. At an additional cost, repeat-back service, personal-delivery-only service, and other options are available.

Repeat-back service requires that the receiving office send the message back to the originating office for comparison. Personal-delivery-only service provides delivery by messenger and requires that the telegram be handed directly to the addressee.

11.31 No special form is needed to send a telegram. If you telephone the message in to the Western Union office, you can type a copy of the message on plain paper for the files. For a nominal charge, you can receive a confirmation copy in the form of a mailgram.

Other Services

11.32 Western Union also operates teletypewriter networks as a communications service. Using this service and a computer, an office can send multiple-address messages, use stored letters and address lists, and use the networks for other communications on a 24-hour basis. Western Union also has available international teletypewriter and international telegram services.

TELEPHONE PROCEDURES

11.33 The ability to use the telephone effectively is essential in today's business office. A knowledge of how to handle incoming and outgoing calls, toll calls, and regular and specialized equipment is a must.

The following tips about general telephone usage should be remembered.

1. Use proper speech habits whenever you use the telephone.
   a. Speak clearly.
   b. Enunciate your words carefully.
   c. Use proper voice inflection; don't speak in a monotone.
   d. Speak at a moderate pace.
   e. Speak directly into the mouthpiece of the telephone.
2. Be courteous and attentive. Become a good listener.
3. Don't keep the other party waiting. If you must leave the telephone for a short time, use the hold button.

4. Avoid slang.
5. Keep a list of emergency numbers near the telephone.
6. Maintain an up-to-date list of telephone numbers that are frequently called.

Incoming Calls

1.34 The following should be considered in handling incoming calls.

1. Always answer the telephone promptly.
2. Identify yourself immediately and completely with your name and your company and/or department.
3. If the call is for someone else, transfer the call or indicate that the person is not available. Ask to take a message.
4. Always be prepared to take a message or copy information.
5. Close the call politely. Replace the receiver gently.
6. If you take a message, be sure it is accurate and legible. Give it to the appropriate person promptly.

Outgoing Calls

1.35 You will probably place outgoing calls—both local and long distance—in the course of your work. These calls may be for yourself or for someone else in the office. Remember the following points when placing outgoing calls.

1. Place your calls at times when those you are calling are most likely to be available.
2. Organize what you are going to say so that you do not waste time. If you are seeking information, plan your questions in advance.
3. Be sure that you have the correct, complete number of the party you are calling. Refer to sources in the office or to the telephone directory. Ask for directory assistance *only* if you are unable to find the correct number yourself. Make a note of that number so you will not have to use directory assistance again.
4. Carefully dial the number of the party you are calling.
5. Allow the telephone to ring a number of times—about ten—before you give up on a call.
6. Identify yourself when the caller answers. State your message clearly and concisely. If necessary, repeat the message.
7. Close the conversation politely; replace the receiver gently.

Toll Calls

1.36 Toll calls (long-distance calls) are generally one of the following types:

1. Dial direct/no operator assistance used
2. Operator-assisted calls
3. Station-to-station calls
4. Person-to-person calls
5. Credit card calls
6. Bill-to-third-number calls
7. Collect calls
8. Conference calls
9. Overseas calls
10. 800 numbers

Dial-Direct/No Operator Assistance Calls

11.37 In most sections of the country, it is now possible to place a long-distance, station-to-station call from residence or business phones by dialing directly. It is even possible in some areas to make international dial direct calls. Dial-direct calls are almost always less expensive than any other type of long-distance call.

To dial direct, do the following:

1. Determine the telephone number of the party you are calling, including the three-digit area code number.
2. Dial "1," the area code, and the complete number.

The charges for a dial-direct call begin when anyone at the called number answers the phone.

Operator-Assisted Calls

11.38 This type of call includes station-to-station calls where operator assistance is needed, person-to-person calls, calls from pay telephones, collect calls, credit card calls, calls billed to another number, or calls on which time and charge information is requested. To place these calls, dial "0," the area code, and the number you are calling. The operator will then come on the line to assist you.

Station-to-Station Calls

11.39 This type of call is used when you will speak to anyone at the number you are calling. It may be placed with or without operator assistance. Charges begin when anyone answers at the called number.

Person-to-Person Calls

11.40 This type of call is used when you wish to speak to a specific person, department, or office. Since this is an operator-assisted call, the charges are higher than for a station-to-station call.

To complete a person-to-person call, dial "0," the area code, then the complete number. When the operator comes on the line, state that you wish to make a person-to-person call and give the name of the party to whom you wish to speak. The charges start only when you begin your conversation with the party you called or with someone else you accept.

Even though the rates are higher than for station-to-station calls, it may be more economical to call person-to-person if you are not sure that the party you wish to talk with will be present. If your party is unavailable, you are not charged for the call.

Credit Card Calls

1.41 People who have telephone system credit cards can place long-distance calls and charge them to their credit card numbers. Credit card calls are operator-assisted calls, but they may be either station-to-station or person-to-person. They are billed at the higher operator-assisted rate.

When you have completed dialing your call, the operator will come on the line for information regarding the type of call you are placing and your credit card number.

Bill-to-Third-Number Calls

1.42 This service is used when you wish to place a long-distance call and transfer the charge to another telephone number. For example, if you place a personal call from your office, you can have the operator charge the cost of the call to your home telephone number. Since this is an operator-assisted call, you are charged a higher rate.

Collect Calls

1.43 Collect calls are those long-distance calls that are charged to the number you are calling. The operator will ask the called party to accept the charges. The called party can, of course, refuse to accept the charges. A higher rate is charged for this operator-assisted call.

Conference Calls

11.44 Using a conference call, you can talk to several people in different locations at the same time. Tell the operator that you wish to make a conference call and give the numbers of the individuals to whom you wish to speak. You should, of course, let the parties you are calling know of the scheduled call in advance so that they will all be available. Conference calls are billed at the higher person-to-person rate since operator assistance is required.

Many companies are discovering that conference calls save time and money by eliminating travel and other expenses. In some areas, it is even possible to hold conferences by telephone with the participants being seen on a television screen.

Overseas Calls

11.45 International Direct Distance Dialing is available to over 35 countries. Check your telephone directory to determine whether such service is available in your area.

If International Direct Distance Dialing is not available, simply tell the operator that you wish to make an overseas call and give the country, name, and telephone number of the party you are calling.

800 Number Calls

11.46 The "800" numbers are usually referred to as WATS (*Wide Area Telecommunications Service*) lines. For companies having 800 numbers, you may dial direct without being charged for the call. The company being called is billed for the call. Many large businesses, hotels, and motels maintain 800 numbers for the convenience of their customers.

Some companies utilize a modified version of WATS. They receive reduced rates for long-distance calls they originate but are not assigned 800 numbers.

Long-Distance Rates

11.47 Rates for long-distance calls are affected by the following:

1. Type of call—station-to-station or operator-assisted.
2. Time of day.
3. Day of the week.
4. Whether or not holiday rates are in effect. On New Year's Day (January 1), July 4, Labor Day (first Monday in September), Thanksgiving, and Christmas Day (December 25), the 5 P.M. to 11 P.M. 35% discount rate applies all day on dial-direct calls.
5. Length of the telephone call.
6. Distance.

Figure 11-2 gives general rate standards for out-of-state long-distance calls.

Dial-Direct Calls One-Minute Rates				Operator-Assisted Calls Three-Minute Rates	
Monday-Friday	Sat.	Sun.		Station-to-Station	Person-to-Person
8 a.m. to 5 p.m. Full Rate				Full Rate All Days All Hours	Full Rate All Days All Hours
5 p.m. to 11 p.m. 35% Discount		35% Discount			
11 p.m. to 8 a.m. 60% Discount					

Figure 11-2

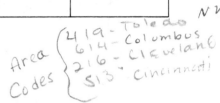

Area Codes { 419 - Toledo   N W
             614 - Columbus
             216 - Cleveland
             513 - Cincinnati }

Local Directory Assistance

11.48 Use directory assistance for local calls only when necessary. Be sure that you have tried to locate the number yourself before you call information. In some areas, the telephone company imposes a charge for directory assistance after the first three or four uses per month.

Long-Distance Directory Assistance

11.49 To determine a telephone number for a city outside your own area, dial "1," the area code for the desired city, and 555-1212. The operator will then give you the number for the party you are calling. Even though there is no extra charge for long-distance directory assistance, you should keep a listing of long-distance numbers frequently called to avoid using directory assistance.

11.50 If you reach a wrong number while placing a long-distance call, dial the operator immediately and explain what happened. You will not be charged for the incorrect call.

11.51 If the connection is poor or you get cut off during a long-distance call, hang up the phone. The person placing the call should then contact the operator and ask that the call be re-established. Charges will be adjusted to reflect the interruption.

Using the Telephone Directory

11.52 In order to find numbers quickly in the telephone directory, remember the following hints:

1. Know the name and correct spelling of the party you are calling.
2. Use the name guides at the top of each page.
3. If two last names are the same, a name having initials only will precede a name having a full first name beginning with the same letter. In other words, initials precede full names.
4. Abbreviations are listed as though they were spelled out in full.
5. Numbers are listed as if spelled in full.
6. The article "the" follows the company name.
7. Company names that include full personal names are transposed (Wilson W W Company).
8. To save space, no punctuation—except apostrophes—appears in the listings.
9. Government listings are found under the appropriate level of government:
   a. Federal government—see United States Government
   b. State government—see state name
   c. County government—see county name
   d. City government—see city name

11.53 You should also refer to the telephone directory for information on dialing instructions, emergency numbers, telephone service and repairs, long-distance rates, area codes, and other general telephone information.

11.54 The Yellow Pages contains an alphabetic listing of advertisers by product or service—from accordions to zippers. Refer to it when you want to find products and services quickly. Many Yellow Pages directories contain a quick reference index at the front that provides a complete alphabetic listing of all headings found in the Yellow Pages.

Area Code/Time Zone Map

11.55 It is important to remember that there are different time zones within the United States and throughout the world. There is a 3-hour time difference between the East and West coasts of the continental United States. Therefore, you should not place a call from one coast to the other unless you are aware of the hours of operation of the business you are calling. For example, you should not place a call from New York at 8 A.M. to a place of business in Los Angeles and expect the offices to be open. Figure 11-3 shows both time zones and area codes within the United States and Canada.

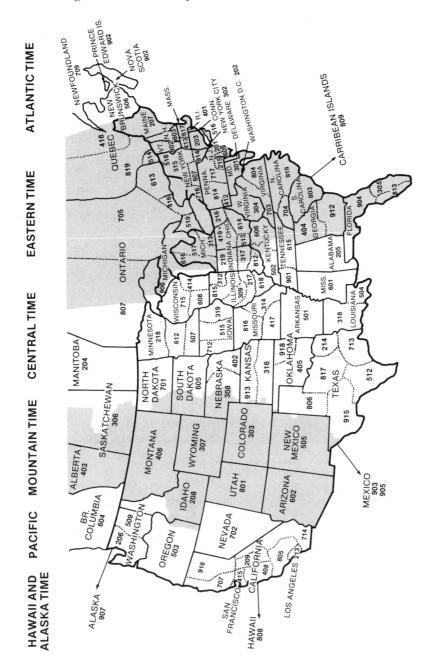

Figure 11-3   Area code/time zone map

NAME _Amy Young_

Self-Check Exercise

SECTION I

Identify the class of postal service—first, second, third, or fourth—likely to be used for the following items.

_____ 1. A package of merchandise weighing 67 pounds

_____ 2. A magazine

_____ 3. A handwritten letter

_____ 4. A circular weighing less than 16 ounces

_____ 5. A typed postal card

_____ 6. A small box of seeds

SECTION II

In the blank to the left, write the name of the special service described.

_____ 1. A letter immediately delivered to the addressee once it reaches its destination

_____ 2. A package paid for by the addressee when delivered

_____ 3. Guaranteed next-day delivery of a package weighing 10 pounds

_____ 4. Used to certify that an item was mailed and delivered; used for important documents that have no value in themselves

_____ 5. Third- and fourth-class mail given preferred handling between post offices

_____ 6. Issued when the sender wishes to have proof that an item was mailed

_____ 7. Provides evidence of mailing and delivery, as well as insurance (up to $10,000) against loss or damage

_____ 8. Letter sent to foreign country on stationery that also serves as the envelope

_____ 9. Used to send money through the mail

_____ 10. Used by businesses to enable customers to respond without paying postage; postage is paid by the business only on cards and envelopes returned

SECTION III

From the list of terms at the right, select the letter of the term that best matches the statement at the left.

__I__ 1. Long-distance calls

__F__ 2. A call made to a specific person

__G__ 3. Charges begin when anyone answers the number called

__A__ 4. The party being called agrees to pay the charges

__D__ 5. The called party automatically pays the charges

__B__ 6. Used to talk to several parties at the same time

__J__ 7. Wide Area Telecommunications Service

__E__ 8. Uses facilities of Western Union and the U.S. Postal Service

__H__ 9. Uses facilities of Western Union only

__C__ 10. A call made without operator assistance

A. Collect call

B. Conference call

C. Dial-direct call

D. 800 numbers

E. Mailgram

F. Person-to-person

G. Station-to-station

H. Telegram

I. Toll calls

J. WATS

SECTION IV

Select the best answer from those given to complete the statement.

__a__ 1. To dial direct, station to station, you must (a) dial "1," the area code, then the complete number; (b) dial "0", the area code, then the complete number; (c) dial "0" and wait for the operator to complete the call.

__a__ 2. Person-to-person calls are (a) more expensive than station-to-station calls, (b) less expensive than station-to-station calls, (c) the same cost as station-to-station calls.

__c__ 3. Charges for long-distance calls are determined by (a) day of the week, (b) how long the conversation lasts, (c) both a and b.

__c__ 4. Long-distance calls are least expensive from (a) 8 A.M. to 5 P.M., (b) 5 P.M. to 11 P.M., (c) 11 P.M. to 8 A.M.

__b__ 5. Use directory assistance (a) when you need a telephone number quickly, (b) only when you cannot find the telephone number elsewhere, (c) when you get a poor connection.

Check your answers in the back of the book.

12 Securing Employment

ACCORDING TO the U.S. Department of Labor statistics, there are around 17 million office jobs available. If you possess the necessary qualifications, finding employment should not be difficult because the outlook for jobs in business offices in the next decade is very favorable. However, your search may be more difficult if you are selective in terms of a specific job, the size of the organization, salary expected, and location.

SOURCES OF JOB INFORMATION AND OPPORTUNITIES

12.1 Once you have completed your training and you possess the necessary basic skills for employment, you should begin your search for a suitable job. There are numerous sources of job information and leads available, including the following:

1. Direct inquiries
2. Friends and relatives
3. Newspaper classified sections
4. Private employment agencies
5. Public employment service agencies
6. School placement services
7. Social agencies
8. Specialized publications
9. Teachers and guidance counselors

12.2 After you have one or more job leads, you should contact the employing firm for an interview. If you telephone the firm to request an appointment for an interview, be sure to speak clearly and courteously. Ask for the correct pronunciation and spelling of the name of the interviewer. Find out the correct time and place of the interview.

A letter of application is frequently used as the initial contact with a prospective employer.

LETTER OF APPLICATION

12.3 A good *letter of application* (see Figure 12-1) is always typewritten and will usually include the following:

```
                                107 Rockton Drive
                                Cleveland, OH 44106
                                May 12, 19--


        Mrs. Ellen Rider
        Personnel Director
        Tele-Vac Corporation
        1406 Dow Circle
        Cleveland, OH 44111

        Dear Mrs. Rider

        Mr. Thomas Delaney, Placement Director of Highland College, has
        told me of your need for a competent secretary in the legal de-
        partment of Tele-Vac Corporation.  Please consider me an appli-
        cant for the position.

        On May 22, I will complete the secretarial program at Highland
        College and will receive an Associate of Arts degree in Secretarial
        Science.  As indicated by the enclosed resume, I have the train-
        ing and the experience needed to make a real contribution to your
        firm.  In addition to the basic secretarial program, my training
        included special emphasis on legal secretarial skills.  I served
        as an intern in the legal office of Harmon, Little, and White
        for a period of six months.  In addition, I plan to enroll in the
        paralegal program at South Cuyahoga College in the fall to further
        my education.

        May I have the opportunity to discuss my qualifications with you
        and the extent to which I could contribute to the success of Tele-
        Vac Corporation.  You may telephone me at 443-6709.

                                Sincerely

                                *Lynda Yang*

                                Lynda Yang


        Enclosure
```

Figure 12-1   Letter of application

1. Your complete address, including a telephone number, so that you can be notified of an interview
2. If possible, the name of a particular person in the company instead of a position (such as Personnel Director)
3. Three paragraphs that
   a. Indicate the particular position for which you are applying and how you learned of it

12

    b. Present your basic qualifications and express the belief that you can make a contribution to the organization

    c. Request an interview

Naturally, the letter of application should present your very best effort. It should be attractive and absolutely free of grammatical, spelling, and punctuation errors. Use a good grade of white bond paper. Make sure that your typewriter gives clear, dark type.

THE RÉSUMÉ

12.4 It is generally recommended that you include a *résumé* (sometimes referred to as a *data sheet*) with the letter of application. The purpose of the résumé is to convey, in as positive and concise a manner as possible, your qualifications for the position you are seeking. In addition to personal information, résumés may include information about the position sought or your career objective, a summary of your educational background and special training, your previous work experience, any activities or accomplishments that might be pertinent to the position you are seeking, and several references.

12.5 The following points should be remembered in developing your résumé.

1. If possible, hold your résumé to one or two pages. Most personnel directors and prospective employers are not impressed by lengthy résumés.

2. Be sure that your résumé is neat and attractive. Use good quality white bond paper and a typewriter with a dark ribbon. While a perfectly typed original copy of a résumé is likely to make the best impression, a clear, clean photocopy is generally acceptable.

   Your résumé should be absolutely free of errors. It should be easy to read and eye-catching in appearance. Avoid large blocks of type. Separate the parts of the résumé with headings for easier reading.

3. Be direct and to the point regarding your past work experience. If you have had no previous paid work experience, list any volunteer experience that would indicate your ability and willingness to work such as assisting teachers at school, teaching Sunday school, or doing volunteer work.

   Include addresses so that your former employers can be contacted by mail if necessary.

4. List awards, honors, and promotions. Be sure to include any accomplishments that emphasize qualities of leadership and scholarship.
5. Include specific educational experiences and travel that furthered your occupational goals or that made you a well-rounded individual.
6. Be honest about your accomplishments and experiences.

Figure 12-2 is an example of a résumé.

Lynda Yang
107 Rockton Drive
Cleveland, OH 44106
Telephone (216) 443-6709

CAREER OBJECTIVE   To secure a responsible office support position with
                        opportunities for growth

EDUCATION

September 1978   Highland College, Cleveland, OH 44115. Will receive
to present   Associate of Arts degree in Secretarial Science on
                        May 22, 1980, with 3.0 average in all course work.

September 1974   Cleveland Central High School, Cleveland, OH 44119.
to June 1978   Majors in business, English, mathematics, and social
                        science. Graduated with honor.

EXPERIENCE

December 1979   Harmon, Little, and White, Attorneys-at-Law, 401 Central
to May 1980   Boulevard, Cleveland, OH 44111. Served as legal secre-
                        tary in Highland College intern program.

September 1979   Highland College Registrar's Office, 3003 College Drive,
to November 1979   Cleveland, OH 44115. Part-time secretary to the Regis-
                        trar while attending school.

June 1978   Dirham Construction Company, 741 Mill Street, Cleveland,
to August 1978   OH 44102. Clerk-typist in the Contract Procurement
                        Department.

ACTIVITIES   President, Highland College Business Club
                        Member of Highland College Student Senate
                        Member of Baptist Student Union
                        Placed fourth in state typewriting contest while attending
                            Cleveland Central High School

REFERENCES   Dr. Elaine Thompson, Professor, Business Education De-
(by permission)   partment, Highland College, 3003 College Drive, Cleveland,
                        OH 44115, (216) 422-6600

                        Miss Wanda Brill, Dirham Construction Company, 741 Mill
                        Street, Cleveland, OH 44102, (216) 427-1632

                        Reverend Dru Wilson, First Baptist Church, 702 Main
                        Street, Cleveland, OH 44106, (216) 435-8945

Figure 12-2 Résumé

THE APPLICATION FORM

12.6 After the prospective employer receives your letter, you may receive an application form or be invited to the company office to complete the form.

Here are some points to remember in completing an application form.

1. If you complete the form at the company office, be sure to take with you
   a. a dependable pen;
   b. your social security number;
   c. a listing of your education and work experience; and
   d. a listing of your references, including their addresses and telephone numbers. (Be sure that you have secured permission from those you are listing.)
2. Read the application form thoroughly before you begin to complete it. Plan your answers as you read through the form.
3. Study each blank before you complete it. You may be asked to print or type the information on the form or you may be specifically told to complete it in your own handwriting. If you complete the form using a pen, print neatly and legibly. Do *not* use a pencil.
4. Follow the directions exactly and complete each blank on the form. Where blanks do not apply to you, draw a line through or write NA (Not Applicable) in the spaces. Answer all questions honestly. If you are asked to state an expected salary, you may indicate a range or that your salary expectations are "open," meaning that this is open for discussion.
5. Proofread the form carefully. Be sure that you have completed each blank and that you have made no errors.
6. Sign and date the form.

12.7 While employers were once free to ask almost any question on the application forms and during interviews, federal and state laws now prohibit questions of the following type:

1. Age
2. Arrest record
3. Height and weight (unless this is an important consideration for the job)
4. Marital status
5. Race or national origin
6. Religion
7. Sex

Application for Employment

TELE-VAC CORPORATION
1406 Dow Circle
Cleveland, OH 44111

An Equal Opportunity Employer

PERSONAL INFORMATION

Name Yang   Lynda   Initial
          Last   First

Date May 28, 19--

Present Address 107 Rockton Drive   Cleveland   OH   44106
                         Street   Town or City   State   ZIP

Phone Number 663-6709   Social Security No. 427-54-7403

Citizen of U.S.? Yes

Position Desired Secretary, Legal Department   Salary Desired Open

In Case of Emergency, Notify Mr. and Mrs. C. W. Yang
                              107 Rockton Drive, Cleveland, OH 44106

EDUCATION

School	Name and Location	Dates Attended From	Dates Attended To	Did You Graduate?	Course
Elementary	Hillsdale Elementary School Cleveland, OH 44119	Sept. 1966	June 1974	Yes	
High School	Cleveland Central High School Cleveland, OH 44119	Sept. 1974	June 1978	Yes	
College or University	Highland College Cleveland, OH 44115	Sept. 1978	Present	In June	Bus., Eng., Math., Soc. Science
Other					

Check Business Courses Taken in School:

X Accounting   X General Business   X Shorthand
__ Business Law   X Office Machines   X Typewriting Legal Secretarial
X Business Math   X Office Practice   __ Other
__ Consumer Economics __ Record Keeping

Typewriting Speed 70 WPM   Shorthand Speed 120 WPM

List Extracurricular Activities and/or Scholastic Honors:
President, Highland College Business Club; Graduated with honor from
Cleveland Central High School; Member of Highland College Student Senate;
Member BSU; Placed fourth in State Typing Contest

EMPLOYMENT

Employed From	To	Company Name and Address	Position	Reason for Leaving
Dec. 1979	May 1980	Harmon, Little, and White 401 Central Boulevard Cleveland, OH 44111	Legal Secretary	Concluded Intern Program
Sept. 1979	Nov. 1979	Highland College 3003 College Drive Cleveland, OH 44115	Registrar's Secretary	Started Intern Program
June 1978	Aug. 1978	Dirham Construction Company 741 Mill Street Cleveland, OH 44102	Clerk-typist	Started School

REFERENCES

Do not list relatives or former employers.

Name	Address	Phone No.	Occupation
Dr. Elaine Thompson	Highland College Cleveland, OH 44115	422-6600	Professor
Miss Wanda Brill	Dirham Construction Co., 741 Mill St., Cleveland, OH	427-1632	Off. Mgr.
Rev. Dru Wilson	First Baptist Church, 702 Main, Cleveland, OH 44106	435-8945	Minister

Are You Currently Employed? No   Date Available for Work June 15, 19--

To the best of my knowledge all of the foregoing information is true and is given voluntarily.

I hereby give permission to contact my references, including previous employers, and to confirm my credentials.

Lynda Yang
          Signature

TO BE COMPLETED BY INTERVIEWER

Interviewed By _____   Date Interviewed _____

Remarks _____

Date Employed _____   Position _____

Department _____   Salary _____

Figure 12-3   Application for employment

The employer cannot ask for your age or date of birth, but can ask if you are between 18 and 65 years of age. If you are not between 18 and 65, you must give your age.

Employers cannot ask you about disabilities or handicaps, nor can they ask you for a specific list of diseases you have had. The employer may, however, ask whether you have a disability—physical or mental—that would interfere with your ability to perform the duties of the position for which you have applied.

Employers cannot require that you attach a photograph to a résumé or application form at any time before you are hired.

Figure 12-3 is an example of a completed application form.

THE EMPLOYMENT TEST

12.8 Depending on the job you are seeking, you may be required to take an employment test. Employment tests for clerical and secretarial positions, for example, may include a typewriting test, a shorthand test, a spelling test, and/or a computation skills test.

12.9 If you take an employment test, remember the following:

1. Ask for some time to warm up on the typewriter so that you may familiarize yourself with the machine.
2. Try to remain calm and relaxed during the test.
3. Use your time effectively, especially if it is a timed test.
4. If you complete the test early, go back over your answers.

THE INTERVIEW

12.10 After the initial screening of applicants through the application form and the employment test, those candidates remaining are usually scheduled for an interview. The interview is an opportunity for you to present your qualifications for the job and to seek specific information about the company and the job. It is an opportunity for the employer to discuss your qualifications and evaluate you personally.

12.11 Remember the following tips:

1. Go alone. Never take a friend or relative along on the interview.
2. Dress appropriately. Do not dress too casually or flashily. It is best to wear clothes that give you a businesslike appearance.
3. Arrive just a few minutes before the scheduled interview time. It is best not to arrive too early and *never* arrive late. Be sure you know in advance where to go and to whom to report.
4. Carry two copies of your résumé in case they are requested.
5. Be sure to carry a reliable pen with you. (If you will be required to

take an employment test at the time of the interview, be sure to carry other needed materials—pencil, eraser, etc.)

6. Before you report for the interview, try to find out as much as you can about the company—its products, size, nature of the business, and so on.
7. Do not carry a lot of things with you that will create clutter.
8. Give your name to the receptionist and indicate with whom you have an appointment. Wait to be told what to do. You may be asked to take a seat until the interviewer is ready for you.
9. Unless you are announced to the interviewer, give your full name clearly and firmly. Shake hands with the interviewer firmly but not overwhelmingly.
10. Never place your personal items (bags, papers, etc.) on the interviewer's desk. Hold them in your lap or place them alongside your chair.
11. Do not chew gum or smoke even if the interviewer indicates that you may.
12. Try to appear relaxed but businesslike throughout the interview. Remember that you have something to offer the company.
13. Let the interviewer take the lead. Answer all questions clearly and fully, but do not elaborate too much. Be sure, however, to answer some questions with more than just a "yes" or "no." The interviewer may be evaluating your ability to respond fully.
14. Do not be hesitant to talk about your accomplishments. Sell yourself, but do not oversell.
15. Do not be afraid to smile. A pleasant expression and a good smile indicate self-confidence.
16. Have some pertinent questions in mind if an opportunity presents itself. Do not be afraid to ask about salary, but do not appear to place too much importance on it. Ask about opportunities for advancement and for additional responsibility.
17. If the matter of salary is not brought up by the interviewer, ask what the salary range is. If you are asked what salary you expect, you might indicate a salary range you have in mind or you might indicate that you would consider what is generally paid by the company for someone of your qualifications and experience.
18. Do not be afraid to ask questions if you are unsure of what the job entails.
19. Be courteous throughout the interview even if you decide that you do not want the job. You might change your mind later or another position may become available with the firm.
20. Watch for an indication that the interview is drawing to a close. Be ready to leave the office as soon as the interview is over.
21. Try to determine what the interviewer's next step will be. Find out if and when you will be notified of the decision.
22. Be sure to thank the interviewer for the opportunity to discuss the

job. If you are interested in the position, indicate that you hope you will be considered favorably.

23. Thank the receptionist on your way out.

THE FOLLOW-UP LETTER

12.12 A day or so after the interview, write a letter thanking the interviewer for the opportunity to discuss your qualifications for the position (see Figure 12-4). If you have decided that you do not wish to be considered further for the job, indicate this and your reasons—you do not believe you are suited for the job, you have found another position, your plans have changed, etc. If you are still interested in the job, indicate this and your belief that you can make a contribution to the company. Be courteous, regardless of your decision. Never burn your bridges behind you.

ADVANCEMENT TIPS

12.13 If you have properly evaluated a position, you should have a good idea of its advancement opportunities and what is required for that advancement. It might require additional training or courses; the ability to assume additional responsibility; or the ability to organize, plan, and supervise. Many companies provide additional training or pay for courses that can help you in your work.

12.14 Here are some techniques for helping you get ahead in your job.

1. Always arrive early or on time for work; never leave early.
2. Be productive; do not waste time, supplies, or energy.
3. Be persistent. See a job through until it is finished.
4. Meet your schedules. Take care of your responsibilities.
5. Do not make excuses for your failures. Resolve not to let them happen again.
6. Do not participate in office gossip.
7. Be loyal and supportive of your supervisors, your employers, and your company.
8. Learn to get along with those with whom you work. Be cooperative, courteous, and considerate.
9. Learn to give and to follow directions. Develop a good memory.
10. Express your ideas and opinions constructively.
11. Do not discuss company matters outside the office.
12. Be dependable—all the time.
13. Be cost conscious.
14. Improve your skills.
15. Leave your personal life at home. Do not bring it to the office.

16. Represent your company well to customers and to the outside world.
17. Be businesslike in your dress, your attitude, and your behavior.
18. Learn as much as you can about the operation of your company.
19. Maintain a positive attitude toward your job. Do not become disgruntled because someone else was selected for a promotion over you.
20. Make every day count. Let your work make a real difference in the success of your company.

---

107 Rockton Drive
Cleveland, OH 44106
May 29, 19--

Mrs. Ellen Rider
Personnel Director
Tele-Vac Corporation
1406 Dow Circle
Cleveland, OH 44111

Dear Mrs. Rider

Thank you for the opportunity to discuss with you yesterday my qualifications for the secretarial position with your firm. I was impressed with your description of the position and with the opportunities that exist. I am certain that the work would be challenging and interesting.

I am very much interested in the job and hope that you feel, as I do, that my training and skills would be useful to your firm. The potential growth of the company and the many opportunities to make a contribution certainly appeal to me.

Please do not hesitate to call me if you need additional information. I hope to hear from you soon regarding your decision.

Sincerely

Lynda Yang

Lynda Yang

Figure 12-4   Follow-up letter

Self-Check Exercise

SECTION I

Indicate whether you agree or disagree with the following statements by writing T (True) or F (False) in the blanks.

_____ 1. If possible, you should address a letter of application to a particular person rather than to a position such as "Personnel Director."

_____ 2. Another name for data sheet is résumé.

_____ 3. A clear, clean photocopy of a résumé is generally acceptable.

_____ 4. You should draw a line or write NA in the blanks on an application form that do not apply to you.

_____ 5. Federal law prohibits employers from asking questions about marital status during an interview or on an application form.

_____ 6. It is acceptable to take a friend along for a job interview, provided the friend waits in the reception area.

_____ 7. Even if the interviewer indicates that you may smoke, it is probably best not to.

_____ 8. If chewing gum helps you relax, you should do so during an interview, especially if you can do it quietly.

_____ 9. You should never bring up the matter of salary with the interviewer since you might be accused of being too concerned with money.

_____ 10. If you decide that you don't want a job you were interviewed for, there is no need to let the employer know about your decision.

SECTION II

In the blanks to the left, write the letter of the most appropriate word or phrase needed to complete the following statements.

_____ 1. It is recommended that the résumé be limited to (a) 2–3 pages, (b) 3–4 pages, (c) 1–2 pages.

_____ 2. A good letter of application will (a) be attractive and free of errors, (b) be prepared on a good grade of bond paper using a typewriter with a dark ribbon, (c) both a and b.

_____ 3. In completing an application form, use a (a) typewriter or pencil, (b) pencil, (c) typewriter or pen.

_____ 4. During an interview, you should place personal items (a) in your lap or alongside your chair, (b) on the interviewer's desk, (c) on the receptionist's desk.

_____ 5. Under *no* circumstances can an employer require you to answer questions about your (a) age, (b) marital status, (c) height and weight.

_____ 6. In reporting for an interview, you should arrive (a) very early, just to be sure that you get there; (b) right on time; (c) just a few minutes before the scheduled time.

_____ 7. During the interview, you should (a) answer all questions with a simple yes or no, (b) let the interviewer take the lead, (c) immediately ask about company benefits and salary.

_____ 8. An application form generally provides spaces for (a) name, address, age, and sex; (b) name, education, and references; (c) name, employment record, and race or national origin.

_____ 9. When you report for the interview, take with you (a) two copies of your résumé and a reliable pen, (b) a portable typewriter in case you have to take a typing test, (c) a list of questions for the interviewer to answer during the interview.

_____ 10. A good letter of application will probably (a) include your complete address and telephone number, (b) be written in your best handwriting, (c) be two pages long.

Check your answers in the back of the book.

13 Reference Sources

THERE ARE a number of reference sources with which office personnel should be familiar. Many of the references should be readily available in the office. Others are available at a public library.

ALMANACS

13.1 Almanacs, generally published on an annual basis, include a wide range of facts and general information on important events of the year, politics, sports, geography, history, statistics, etc.

CBS News Almanac. Maplewood, N.J.: Hammond, Inc. (Covers opinion polls, events, history, government, travel and transportation, census information, nations, sports, and prizes and awards.)

Information Please Almanac. New York: Viking Press. (Covers politics, sports, taxes, geography, vital statistics, and social and political conditions.)

Wallechinsky, David, and Wallace, Irving. *The Peoples Almanac.* Garden City, N.Y.: Doubleday & Co., Inc., 1975. (Contains little-known facts about the United States, nations, history, science, health, sports, and honors.)

Wallechinsky, David, and Wallace, Irving. *The Peoples Almanac 2.* New York: William Morrow & Co., Inc., 1978. (Entirely new; little-known facts.)

World Almanac and Book of Facts. New York: Newspaper Enterprise Association, Inc. (Includes a wide variety of information on education, events, sports, population, U.S. government organizations, and political activities.)

BIOGRAPHICAL BOOKS

13.2 Biographical publications supply general information about notable individuals including personal background, education, occupation or profession, personal information, accomplishments, and honors. Many are revised and updated on a regular basis.

Dictionary of American Biography. New York: Charles Scribner's Sons, 1977. (Information about notable nonliving Americans.)

Webster's Biographical Dictionary. Springfield, Mass.: G. & C. Merriam Co., 1976. (Identifies notable persons from all periods.)

Who's Who. New York: St. Martin's Press, Inc., 1978. (Directory of notable people, mostly British.)

Who's Who in America. 40th ed. 2 vols. Chicago: Marquis Who's Who Books, Inc., 1978. (Information about notable living Americans.)

Other *Who's Who* publications include *Who's Who of American Women, Who's Who in Finance and Industry, Who's Who in Government*, and others covering particular geographical areas.

DICTIONARIES

13.3 Dictionaries are an essential part of the reference library for office workers. Dictionaries range in size from small pocket editions to the complete, unabridged volumes. Dictionaries generally provide the following: spelling, syllabication, pronunciation, part of speech, origin of the word, definitions, uses, capitalization, synonyms, and irregular word forms. Specialized dictionaries deal with the vocabulary of certain professions (legal, medical, engineering, etc.), synonyms, and special word lists.

The American Heritage Dictionary of the English Language. Boston: Houghton Mifflin Co., 1979. (Clear, understandable definitions for over 155,000 entries.)

Funk & Wagnalls Standard Desk Dictionary. Scranton, Pa.: Funk & Wagnalls Co., dist. by Harper & Row Publishers, 1977. (Desk-sized reference book for correct spelling, syllabication, etc.)

The Legal Word Book. Boston: Houghton Mifflin Co., 1978. (A quick reference guide to spelling 20,000 legal words, legal forms and citations, and directories of U.S. counties, courts, and embassies.)

Leslie, Louis A. *20,000 Words.* 7th ed. New York: Gregg Division, McGraw-Hill Book Co., 1977. (A pocket-sized book for checking spelling and word division.)

The Medical and Health Sciences Word Book. Boston: Houghton Mifflin Co., 1977. (A guide to spelling and division of over 60,000 medical terms, drug trade names, surgical instruments, medical signs and symbols, and weights and measures.)

The Random House College Dictionary. New York: Random House Inc., 1975. (College edition of the Random House Dictionary.)

The Right Word. Boston: Houghton Mifflin Co., 1978. (A concise thesaurus that lists synonyms, antonyms, and differentiates between related words.)

Roget, Peter M. *Roget's International Thesaurus.* 4th ed. Scranton, Pa.: Thomas Y. Crowell Co., dist. by Harper & Row Publishers, 1977. (A guide to the right word choice.)

Webster's Collegiate Thesaurus. Springfield, Mass.: G. & C. Merriam Co., 1976. (A desk-sized guide to choosing the right word.)

13

Webster's New Collegiate Dictionary. Springfield, Mass.: G. & C. Merriam Co., 1977. (Desk-sized spelling guide.)

Webster's Third New International Dictionary. Springfield, Mass.: G. & C. Merriam Co., 1976. (Unabridged form.)

The Word Book. Boston: Houghton Mifflin Co., 1976. (A guide to the spelling, syllabication, and pronunciation of more than 40,000 commonly used words.)

DIRECTORIES

13.4 Directories provide alphabetical listings of the names and addresses of people in a particular business, industry, or profession in a given geographical area. Directories provide assistance in finding the names, addresses, and telephone numbers of persons or companies and also give information about company officers and products.

City directories. These directories generally list names, addresses, and occupations of city residents.

Congressional Directory. Washington, D.C.: Superintendent of Documents, U.S. Government Printing Office. (Lists members of Congress and Executive Department personnel.)

Dun & Bradstreet Ratings and Reports. New York: Dun & Bradstreet, Inc. (Lists credit ratings of firms.)

Fortune Directory. New York: Fortune Magazine. (Lists major firms in the United States by sales, assets, and net profits.)

Moody's Manuals. New York: Moody's Investors Service, Inc. (Gives financial information on investment companies including transportation, public utilities, banks and finance, and government.)

Rand McNally Bankers Directory. Chicago: Rand McNally & Co. (Provides names of bank officers and directors for all banks, foreign and domestic.)

Standard & Poor's Register of Directors and Executives. New York: Standard & Poor's Corp. (Gives information on directors of corporations in the United States and Canada.)

Telephone directories. These directories list telephone subscribers by name and address.

U.S. Government Manual. Washington, D.C.: National Archives and Records Service, General Services Administration. (Describes the purposes and programs of most government agencies and lists key officials.)

ENCYCLOPEDIAS

13.5 Encyclopedias provide information on a wide variety of subjects. General encyclopedias provide brief coverage of many topics; specialized encyclopedias provide broader coverage of fewer topics in a specific area.

Collier's Encyclopedia. 24 vols. New York: Collier, MacMillan Educational Corp., 1979. (A useful, readable encyclopedia.)

Encyclopedia Americana. 30 vols. New York: Grolier Educational Corp., 1978. (Standard, comprehensive, 30-volume encyclopedia.)

The Encyclopedia of Banking and Finance. 7th rev. ed. New York: Bankers Publishing Co., 1973. (Defines and explains banking terms.)

The International Encyclopedia of the Social Sciences. 17 vols. New York: The Macmillan Co., 1968. (Several volumes dealing with politics, history, economics, penology, ethics, and psychology.)

The New Columbia Encyclopedia. 4th ed. New York: Columbia University Press, 1975. (A concise, one-volume general encyclopedia covering 50,000 articles.)

The New Encyclopaedia Britannica. 15th ed. 30 vols. Chicago: Encyclopaedia Britannica, Inc. (Standard 30-volume encyclopedia with yearly updating supplement.)

GENERAL REFERENCE SOURCES

13.6 There are a number of publications that give information regarding shipping and postal rates, hotel and motel rates, geographical locations, reference sources, etc. Many of these publications are issued on a regular basis.

Bullinger's Postal and Shipper's Guide for the United States and Canada. Westwood, N.J.: Bullinger's Guides, Inc. (Contains listings of post offices and railroad stations, railroad lines, and delivery points.)

Directory of Business and Financial Sources. 7th ed. New York: Special Libraries Association, 1976. (Lists business and financial services by scope, type, frequency of publications, format, and price.)

Encyclopedia of Business Information Sources. 3rd ed. 2 vols. Detroit: Gale Research Co., 1976. (Record of sourcebooks, periodicals, organizations, directories, handbooks, bibliographies, and other sources of information.)

Hotel and Motel Red Book. New York: American Hotel Association Directory Corp. (Lists hotels and motels alphabetically by city and state giving location, room information, and room rates.)

Johnson, H. Webster. *How to Use the Business Library.* 4th ed. Cincinnati: South-Western Publishing Co., 1972. (Lists sources of all types of business information.)

Leonard's Guide. New York: G. R. Leonard & Co., Inc. (Contains rates and routes for freight, express, and parcel post.)

National ZIP Code Directory. Washington, D.C.: Superintendent of Documents, U.S. Government Printing Office. (Lists post offices and ZIP Codes.)

Official Airline Guide. Oak Brook, Ill.: Official Airline Guides, Inc. (Comprehensive listing of all flight information.)

Postal Manual. Washington, D.C.: Superintendent of Documents, U.S. Government Printing Office. (Provides comprehensive postal information.)

Rand McNally Commercial Atlas and Marketing Guide. Chicago: Rand McNally & Co. (Provides general geographical and statistical information.)

GRAMMAR AND STYLE BOOKS

13.7 There are many occasions when it is necessary to determine correct grammar or writing style. Some rules and interpretations vary from one reference source to another. A pattern of consistency should be selected and used in the office.

Fowler, Henry W. *Dictionary of Modern English Usage.* 2nd ed. New York: Oxford University Press, Inc., 1965. (Includes definitions of terms and essays on the use and misuse of words and expressions, parts of speech, etc.)

A Manual of Style. 12th ed., rev. Chicago: University of Chicago Press, 1969. (A standard handbook for those preparing typewritten manuscript for printers.)

U.S. Government Printing Office: Style Manual. Rev. ed. Washington, D.C.: U.S. Government Printing Office, 1973. (Typographical rules followed in government printing.)

Words Into Type. 3rd ed. Englewood Cliffs, N.J.: Prentice-Hall, Inc. 1974. (A comprehensive style manual for writers, editors, and the print media.)

The Written Word. Boston: Houghton Mifflin Co., 1977. (A concise guide to writing, usage, and style.)

INDEXES

13.8 Indexes list the contents of books and periodicals and are used to locate information on particular subjects. Indexes generally list titles of books and articles, periodicals, date of publication, and publishers. Most of these indexes are published at least annually.

Ayer Directory of Publications. Philadelphia: Ayer Press. (Contains information on newspapers and periodicals in the United States, its territories, and Canada.)

Books in Print, U.S.A. New York: R. R. Bowker Co. (Provides information about all books, including author, title, price, publisher, and year of publication.)

Business Books in Print. New York: R. R. Bowker Co. (Information on in-print business books available in the United States; covers banking, advertising, research, and other subjects.)

Business Education Index. New York: Delta Pi Epsilon Fraternity and Gregg Division, McGraw-Hill Book Co. (Provides author and subject listings of business education articles, publications, and studies.)

Business Periodical Index. New York: The H. W. Wilson Co. (Index to periodicals in a number of specialized areas including accounting, advertising, and banking.)

Cumulative Book Index. New York: The H. W. Wilson Co. (Information on books, scholarly pamphlets, proceedings and selected periodicals in the English language published by trade publishers, university presses, etc.)

Education Index. New York: The H. W. Wilson Co. (Provides listing of publications in education.)

The New York Times Index. New York: The New York Times Co. (Listings by subject, title, person, and organization of all articles appearing in the *New York Times*.)

Reader's Guide to Periodical Literature. New York: The H. W. Wilson Co. (Provides listing of articles appearing in a wide range of general subjects and periodicals by subject and author.)

OFFICE HANDBOOKS AND TEXTS

13.9 Information on office procedures and practices can be found in a number of handbooks and textbooks.

Anderson, Ruth I., *et al. The Administrative Secretary: Resource.* 3rd ed. New York: Gregg Division, McGraw-Hill Book Co., 1976. (Secretarial resource guide.)

Doris, Lillian, and Miller, Bessie May. *Complete Secretary's Handbook.* 4th ed. Englewood Cliffs, N.J.: Prentice-Hall, Inc., 1977. (Outlines the tasks and responsibilities of the secretary.)

Hanna, J. Marshall, Popham, Estelle L., and Tilton, Rita Sloan. *Secretarial Procedures and Administration.* 7th ed. Cincinnati: South-Western Publishing Co., 1978. (Textbook for the secretary.)

House, Clifford R., and Koebele, Appolonia M. *Reference Manual for Office Personnel.* 5th ed. Cincinnati: South-Western Publishing Co., 1970. (Reference sourcebook.)

Nanassy, Louis C., Selden, William, and Lee, Jo Ann. *Reference Manual for Office Workers.* Encino, Calif.: Glencoe Publishing Co., 1977. (A comprehensive office reference manual.)

Sabin, William A. *The Gregg Reference Manual.* 5th ed. New York: Gregg Division, McGraw-Hill Book Co., 1977. (Reference source for secretarial procedures.)

Whalen, Doris H. *The Secretary's Handbook.* 3rd ed. New York: Harcourt Brace Jovanovich, Inc., 1978. (Reference manual for the office.)

QUOTATIONS SOURCEBOOKS

13.10   Quotations sourcebooks are handy references for the authors of both familiar and not-so-familiar quotations. These books may list quotations by author or by the subject of the quotation.

Bartlett, John. *Bartlett's Familiar Quotations.* 14th ed. Boston: Little, Brown, and Co., 1968. (A collection of passages, phrases, and proverbs traced to their sources in ancient and modern literature.)

International Encyclopedia of Quotations. Rev. ed. Garden City, N.Y.: Doubleday & Co., Inc., 1978. (Desk-sized quotation sourcebook.)

Self-Check Exercise

SECTION I

Match the reference source with the type of information it supplies.

_____ 1. Supplies general information about notable individuals

_____ 2. Published on an annual basis; includes wide range of facts and information

_____ 3. Lists titles of books and articles, authors, periodicals, and publishers

_____ 4. Provides general or specialized coverage of wide variety of subjects; usually in more than one volume

_____ 5. Provides alphabetical listing of names and addresses of persons or businesses

A. Almanac

B. Biographical publication

C. Dictionary

D. Directory

E. Encyclopedia

F. Index

SECTION II

In the blanks, write the letter of the reference source for the information needed.

_____	1. Information needed to reserve overnight accommodations on a trip
_____	2. The postage rates for second-class mail
_____	3. The winner of last year's World Series
_____	4. The address of a person in a large city
_____	5. The freight rate for a package to be sent to another state
_____	6. Information about a notable British citizen
_____	7. The name of the publisher of a best-selling book
_____	8. The author of a famous saying
_____	9. The credit rating of a company
_____	10. The correct way to prepare manuscript for a printer

A. *Who's Who*

B. *World Almanac and Book of Facts*

C. *Dun & Bradstreet Ratings and Reports*

D. City directory

E. *Postal Manual*

F. *A Manual of Style*

G. *Books in Print, U.S.A.*

H. *Reader's Guide to Periodical Literature*

I. *Bartlett's Familiar Quotations*

J. *Leonard's Guide*

K. *Hotel and Motel Red Book*

Check your answers in the back of the book.

Answers to Self-Check Exercises

UNIT 1   PUNCTUATION

TO: Marilyn Flescher, Budget Director
FROM: Richard Riley, Regional Sales Manager
DATE: January 16, 1980
SUBJECT: Evaluation, Salaries, and Bonuses

After the recent sales conference, Mr. Wilson, the National Sales Manager, asked each regional sales office to present ideas for improvement in the following areas: (1) evaluation, (2) salaries, and (3) bonuses. He also asked that our ideas be reported no later than February 15, 1980. The purpose of this memo, Marilyn, is to secure specific, concise information that will help me complete the report.

In his address to the conference, Mr. Wilson said, "We need accurate data to ensure that each representative's work is evaluated fairly." Since this is the case, I wonder if you can supply me with a copy of the incentive plan—or is it referred to as the "bonus plan"—which you presented at the conference. Did your report include employees covered? employee cost? company cost?

Can you also supply me with first-, second-, and third-quarter salary and bonus figures for those employees assigned to our regional office? I suspect that these figures, for example, will clearly show that over 35 representatives exceeded $20,000 in salary and bonuses.

In a recent issue of Financial Weekly, an article entitled "Bonuses and Employee Morale" insisted there was a direct, positive correlation between the two. In discussions with other regional managers, the same correlation was indicated; nevertheless, I am not sure this is always true. Perhaps the information you supply to me will change my mind. Seeing is believing.—Horatio

UNIT 2   CAPITALIZATION

1. She, Columbia University
2. After, Air National Guard, Langley's Department Store
3. Jennifer, Middle West, Boston
4. Consider, Rice, India
5. The United States Senate, Memorial Day

6. The National Business Club, Catalogue
7. The, "Today's Inflation, Tomorrow's Recession," *Chicago Herald,* Sunday, January
8. While, Ms. Andrews, English
9. My, Larry White, Spanish-American War
10. In Astronomy II, Saturn, Earth
11. Each
12. His, General Rudolph, Bible
13. Do
14. The, China, Mexico, Hungary
15. My, mid-July

UNIT 3   NUMBERS

1. 47
2. 10
3. Twenty-seven
4. 13
5. May 13
6. ten, 4:30
7. Fifth
8. $380
9. 65; 48 years, 3 months
10. 10 × 15
11. one third
12. 20%
13. Ninetieth
14. First
15. 11
16. 30,000
17. 20
18. One
19. 16
20. 65

UNIT 4   ABBREVIATIONS

1. Yes
2. No (Colonel)
3. No (Mr.)
4. Yes
5. Yes
6. No (LL.D.)
7. No (B.S.)
8. Yes
9. No (M.A.)
10. Yes
11. No (Ed.D.)
12. Yes
13. Yes
14. Yes
15. No (Central Intelligence Agency)
16. Yes
17. No (SEC)
18. No (Apr.)
19. Yes
20. No (Mon.)
21. No (Thurs.)
22. Yes
23. Yes
24. Yes
25. Yes
26. Yes
27. Yes
28. No (cwt.)
29. Yes
30. No (bbl.)
31. Yes
32. No (m)
33. Yes
34. Yes
35. No (°C)
36. Yes
37. Yes

38. Yes	49. Yes
39. No (optical character recognition)	50. Yes
	51. No (cost, insurance, and freight)
40. Yes	
41. No (Calif.)	52. Yes
42. Yes	53. Yes
43. No (Iowa)	54. Yes
44. Yes	55. Yes
45. No (Mass. and MA)	56. No (free on board)
46. Yes	57. Yes
47. No (Mo. and MO)	58. Yes
48. No (Tex. and TX)	59. Yes
	60. Yes

UNIT 5   GRAMMAR

Section I

1. Wow (int); team (n); easily (adv); championship (adj)
2. They (pro); because (conj); were told (v)
3. In (prep); my (pro); job (n); rarely (adv)
4. Marilyn (n); fastest (adj); on (prep)
5. police (n); led (v); into (prep); quiet (adj)

Section II

1. faster, fastest	6. which
2. his	7. practices
3. have	8. Whom
4. are	9. she
5. his	10. her

UNIT 6   WORD DIVISION AND HYPHENATION

Section I

1. com-plete	6. self-addressed
2. slapped	7. ten-tacle
3. ab-solutely	8. stimu-late
4. trip-ping	9. evalu-ation
5. fall-ing	10. through

Section II

1. No (into)	4. No (Mrs. Harriet/Stowe)
2. No (ide-alistically)	5. No (NAACP)
3. No (ma-nipulate)	6. No (evan-gelical)

7. Yes
8. No (wrapped)
9. Yes
10. Yes

Section III

1. grandfather
3. trade-in value
4. self-control
7. upstanding
8. blue-green water
10. predetermine

UNIT 7   SPELLING AND WORD CHOICE

Section I

1. antitrust
2. bipartisan
3. intrastate
4. misappropriate
5. predetermine
6. transport
7. sleepless
8. fashionable
9. measurement
10. joyful

Section II

1. receive
2. seat of government
3. location
4. financial
5. at an earlier time
6. a grill
7. workers
8. in the same place
9. legal
10. if

Section III

1. achievement
2. allotment
3. arrears
4. benefited
5. breakage
6. budgetary
7. cancellation
8. congratulate
9. creditor
10. deductible
11. depreciate
12. endorsement
13. exaggerate
14. grievance
15. hazard
16. incorporate
17. judgment
18. ledger
19. likelihood
20. maintenance
21. preferable
22. recommendation
23. remittance
24. sincerely
25. taxable
26. tentative
27. unfamiliar
28. unique
29. warranty
30. wherefore

Section IV

1. swimmers
2. switches
3. rallies
4. journeys
5. shelves
6. potatoes
7. oxen
8. women
9. moose
10. fathers-in-law

UNIT 8   TYPING TECHNIQUES
Section I

1. E
2. F
3. D
4. C
5. I
6. A
7. H
8. J
9. G
10. B

Section II

1. agenda
2. Interoffice memos
3. minutes
4. news release
5. intinerary
6. bar, circle, line
7. Invoices
8. purchase order
9. correcting typewriter
10. proofreading

UNIT 9   BUSINESS LETTERS
AND OFFICE COMMUNICATIONS
Section I

1. F
2. G
3. C
4. D
5. I
6. M
7. H
8. A
9. K
10. E
11. J
12. B
13. L

Section II

5 Attention line
8 Body
10 Company name
9 Complimentary close
17 Copy notation
2 Date
15 Enclosure notation
4 Inside address
3 Mailing notation
18 Postscript
1 Printed letterhead
14 Reference initials

6 Salutation
16 Separate cover notation
11 Signature

7 Subject line
13 Title
12 Typed name

Section III

1. 9
2. 10
3. 6
4. 3
5. 5

6. 7
7. 2
8. 4
9. 1
10. 8

UNIT 10   BUSINESS REPORTS

Section I

1. outline
2. table of contents
3. title page
4. index
5. footnote

6. bibliography
7. letter of transmittal
8. appendix
9. introduction
10. text

Section II

1. Roman
2. Two
3. double
4. single
5. 1

6. $1\frac{1}{2}$
7. single
8. triple
9. Roman
10. summary

UNIT 11   USING COMMUNICATIONS SERVICES

Section I

1. fourth
2. second
3. first

4. third
5. first
6. third

Section II

1. special delivery
2. COD
3. express mail
4. certified mail
5. special handling

6. certificate of mailing
7. registered mail
8. aerogrammes
9. postal money order
10. business reply mail

Section III

1. I
2. F
3. G
4. A
5. D

6. B
7. J
8. E
9. H
10. C

Section IV

1. A
2. A
3. C

4. C
5. B

UNIT 12   SECURING EMPLOYMENT

Section I

1. T
2. T
3. T
4. T
5. T

6. F
7. T
8. F
9. F
10. F

Section II

1. C
2. C
3. C
4. A
5. B

6. C
7. B
8. B
9. A
10. A

UNIT 13   REFERENCE SOURCES

Section I

1. B
2. A
3. F

4. E
5. D

Section II

1. K
2. E
3. B
4. D
5. J

6. A
7. G
8. I
9. C
10. F

Glossary

abstract   a summary of the important points of an article or text

accrual   something that increases

acquisition   something that is acquired; an addition to a category or group

actuary   one who calculates insurance risks and premiums

adjudication   hearing and settling a case by judicial procedure

affidavit   a written statement made under oath before a notary public or other authorized person

amortization   the process of writing off expenditures by prorating over a period of time

annuity   the annual interest or dividend on an investment

appraisal   the expert or official valuation of something, as for taxation

arbitration   the process of settling disputes in which the parties agree to abide by the decision of a third party

arrears   an unpaid, overdue debt

assessment   an estimate of the value of property for taxation

asset   something of value that is owned

auditor   one who verifies the financial records of a business or other institution

beneficiary   one who receives benefits from an insurance policy, will, or other settlement

bimonthly   once every two months

bona fide   authentic; genuine; in good faith

broker   one who acts as an agent in the buying and selling of merchandise or securities

capital   any form of wealth used or available for use in the accumulation of more wealth; the net worth of a business

coinsurance   insurance held jointly with others

collateral   property used as security for a loan or other obligation

commodity   something useful that can be turned to advantage; a trade item that can be transported, especially an agricultural or mining product

comptroller   one who audits accounts and supervises the financial affairs of a corporation or governmental body (also controller)

conglomerate   a corporation composed of previously independent companies in unrelated businesses

consignment   goods or cargo given to another for sale or custody

consortium   a group of financial institutions that pool their reserves in a venture requiring extensive financial resources

contingency   a possibility or future emergency that must be prepared for

contract   an agreement between two or more parties that is enforceable by law

convertible   capable of being exchanged for something else

conveyance   the transfer of property from one person to another, usually by a deed

creditor   one to whom a debt is owed

data   organized information used for analysis or as the basis for a decision

debenture   a bond backed only by the credit standing of the issuer; no assets are pledged as security

debtor   one who owes something to another

deficit   financial condition that occurs when expenditures exceed revenue

denomination   a class of units having specified values

depreciation   a decrease or loss in value because of wear, age, or other causes

disbursement   money paid out; an expenditure

endorse   to sign the back of a check, money order, or stock certificate transferring its ownership, usually in exchange for the cash value stated on its face

endowment   a donation of funds or property to an institution, individual, or group that will serve as a source of income

entrepreneur   one who organizes, operates, and assumes the risks for a business venture

equity   the value of a business or property after any mortgage or other liability has been deducted

escrow   a document held by a third person until certain conditions are met

executor   one who is named in a will to carry out the terms of the will

expenditure   an amount spent; an expense

fiduciary   one who holds something in trust for another

foreclosure   the legal procedure by which a mortgage is settled or resolved

franchise   a binding arrangement between a manufacturer and a distributor or dealer to sell the manufacturer's products on an exclusive-territory basis

grantor   one who transfers property by deed

grievance   a complaint often arising from misunderstanding

guaranty   an agreement by which one person agrees to pay or fulfill another's obligation

incorporate   to form a corporation

indebtedness   the state of owing something to another

infringement an encroachment, as of a right

injunction a court order forbidding the performance of a certain act

intangibles assets that cannot be seen, precisely defined, or identified

invalid null; legally worthless

inventory a detailed list of things in one's possession; a periodic check of all goods and materials on hand

investment property or other possessions purchased for the future income or benefit they provide

invoice a bill; a list of goods shipped or services rendered, with a detailed accounting of all costs

jobber one who works on a piecework basis; a middleman who buys from a manufacturer and sells to retailers

judgment a formal or court decision creating or affirming an obligation

jurisdiction authority or control

larceny the theft of another's personal property

lease a contract for the use or occupation of property in exchange for rent

lessee one who holds a lease; a tenant

lessor one who rents property under a lease; a landlord

levy to impose or collect a tax

liability something that is owed; a debt

libel any written or visual statement that ridicules or defames one's character; any slighting statement

license permission to do or own something; a document that serves as proof of permission

lien the right to hold the property of a debtor as security for a debt

liquidate to settle a debt; to wind up the affairs of a business by paying off all debts and distributing remaining assets among the owners

litigation legal proceedings; a lawsuit

lobby to attempt to influence lawmakers to pass, defeat, or amend pending legislation

manifest an itemized list of cargo

maturity the date on which a note, bill, or bond is payable

merchandise goods available for sale or purchase

merger the consolidation of two or more business interests or corporations

monopoly the exclusive control of an operation that results in lack of competition and control of prices

mortgage a claim on property by a creditor as security for the payment of a debt

mortgagee one who holds a mortgage

mutual fund a company that sells shares to investors and uses this capital to invest in other companies

negotiable   capable of being transferred from one person to another, usually by endorsement

notary public   one who is legally authorized to certify documents, take affidavits, and administer oaths

ordinance   a law or regulation, especially one enacted by a city government

partnership   an agreement between two or more persons to co-own a business for profit

patent   the grant to an inventor for the sole right to make, use, and sell an invention for a period of 17 years

policyholder   one who holds an insurance policy or contract

portfolio   a detailed list of the investments, securities, and commercial paper owned

postdated   to date a document as of a later date than the actual one

premium   the amount paid to obtain a loan or an insurance policy

principal   a debt, upon which interest is calculated

probate   the legal process of proving validity of a will

proprietor   the owner or owner-manager of a business

pro rata   in proportion

prospectus   a formal document summarizing the information about securities offering

proxy   a written authorization enabling a stockholder to transfer voting rights

quarterly   occurring at regular intervals of three months

quitclaim   a deed transferring the title, right, or claim to property to another

realty   real estate

receivables   assets representing the total amounts due from others

receivership   the office or functions of one who takes custody of property or funds for another

remittance   the money or credit sent to another

renegotiate   to revise the original terms of a contract in order to limit or get back excess profits gained by the contractor

requisition   a written request for something that is needed

rescind   to abolish or repeal

respondent   one who replies to legal claims; a defendant

retroactive   applying to a previous time period

revenue   income from all sources

semiannual   occurring twice a year

shareholder   one who owns or holds stock

sinking fund   a plan in which money is periodically deposited with a trustee for the repayment of a bond issue

solvent   able to pay debts as they become due

subpoena   a court order requiring a person to appear in court to give testimony

subrogation   the substitution of one person for another

survivorship the right of a surviving partner or joint owner to the entire assets that were originally jointly owned

tangibles assets that are visible and capable of being touched

trustee one who holds legal title to property in order to manage it for another

underwriter one who guarantees the purchase of a full issue of stocks or bonds

violation failure to fulfill one's duties or obligations

voucher a document that proves that the terms of a transaction were met

warranty a legal promise by a seller that the goods or property are as represented or will be as promised

wholesaler one who sells goods in large quantities, usually for resale by a retailer

yield the profit or return from an investment

Index